PRA]
DADS BEHA

"With moving stories beautifully told, *Dads Behaving DADLY 2* is a book all parents can relate to. It's a clear reflection that manhood has evolved, shedding the limitations and bravado of the past in favor of embracing the emotional roller coaster of raising children."

-Josh Levs, Author, *All In: How Our Work-First Culture Fails Dads, Families, and Businesses—And How We Can Fix It Together*

***

"I love everything about *Dads Behaving DADLY 2*. I love the emotions the stories engender in me. I love the diversity of the essayists and of their stories. I love the images of kids with their dads, laughing, crying, playing, and pooping. I have always been proud to consider myself a dad first, above all else, and I am warmed by reading the joy of so many other dads who feel the same."

- Harley A. Rotbart, M.D., Professor and Vice Chair Emeritus of Pediatrics University of Colorado School of Medicine and author of *No Regrets Parenting*, http://www.harleyrotbart.com

***

"*Dads Behaving DADLY 2* vividly captures the experiences, responsibilities and the opportunities today's fathers are confronting - and thriving at. The stories add tremendously to one of the great unfolding narratives in our contemporary culture --- the victories of today's fathers in their pursuit to be seen and accepted as 'whole persons.'"

- Prof. Brad Harrington, Executive Director, Boston College Center for Work & Family

"This book is chock full of authors literally rewriting the narrative of what it means to be a modern father. Be touched and inspired by their variety – whether it's a glimpse into a moment when a dad shares the same worries as mom, or a new raucous tool-wielding approach to parenthood that seems uniquely suited to dad. Together they weave a wonderful tapestry of *Dads Behaving DADLY*."

- Jessica DeGroot, Founder and President, ThirdPath Institute–supporting men and women, as parents and leaders, to follow an integrated approach to work and family.

***

"A collection of heartwarming stories that encouraged me to reflect on my experiences as a dad and left me with tears in my eyes and a smile on my face."

- Josh Spicer, http://daddyengine.net

***

"I smiled, I laughed, I shed a tear, I cried a bit, then I smiled all over again."

- Zachary Crabtree, www.yourefunnydaddy.com

***

"Writing my story for the first *Dads Behaving DADLY* book was a juxtaposition of triumph and defeat as I relived the struggles of my role as a father coupled with my success in breaking through society's stereotype of dads!"

- Sean Rose

“At first I was shy to share my experiences, then honored to be selected for the first *Dads Behaving DADLY* book. I proudly display it on my bookshelf as a testament of brotherhood and my time as an at-home dad.”

- James Kline, Vice-President, National At-Home Dad Network

***

“To be in a book that is a collection of stories from dads that are so different personally but are unified by the single commonality of fatherhood is a humbling experience. Being selected to be a part of the book just made me more proud to be able to share my point of view. To have dads read my words and to come up to me and tell me my story helped change their perspective is powerful beyond words. While these stories may just be words on a page to some, they are stories that remind us just how important our role as dad can be to our children.”

- Chris Bernholdt, www.dadncharge.com

***

“It was very affirming, as a father and a writer, to be a part of something as worthwhile and meaningful as *Dads Behaving DADLY*. I am proud to be a part of this brotherhood of fathers.”

- Matthew Green, www.worldsluckiestman.com

Dads Behaving DADLY 2

72 More Truths, Tears and Triumphs of Modern Fatherhood

Edited By
Hogan Hilling & Al Watts

10% of the royalties from this book are being donated to the Oren Miller Dad 2.0 Scholarship Fund, which provides money to help dad bloggers attend the Annual Dad 2.0 Summit.
Learn more at **www.CrowdRise.com/2016MillerGrants** and follow them **@Dad2Summit**.

Published by Motivational Press, Inc.
1777 Aurora Road
Melbourne, Florida, 32935
www.MotivationalPress.com

www.DadsBehavingDadly.com

Cover photo by: Brent Almond, www.DesignerDaddy.com

Manufactured in the United States of America.

ISBN: 978-1-62865-195-9

Cover Photo Credits

A special thanks to these dads for sharing their photos for the cover of this book:

Jameson Mercier

Michael Cruse

Christopher Sansone

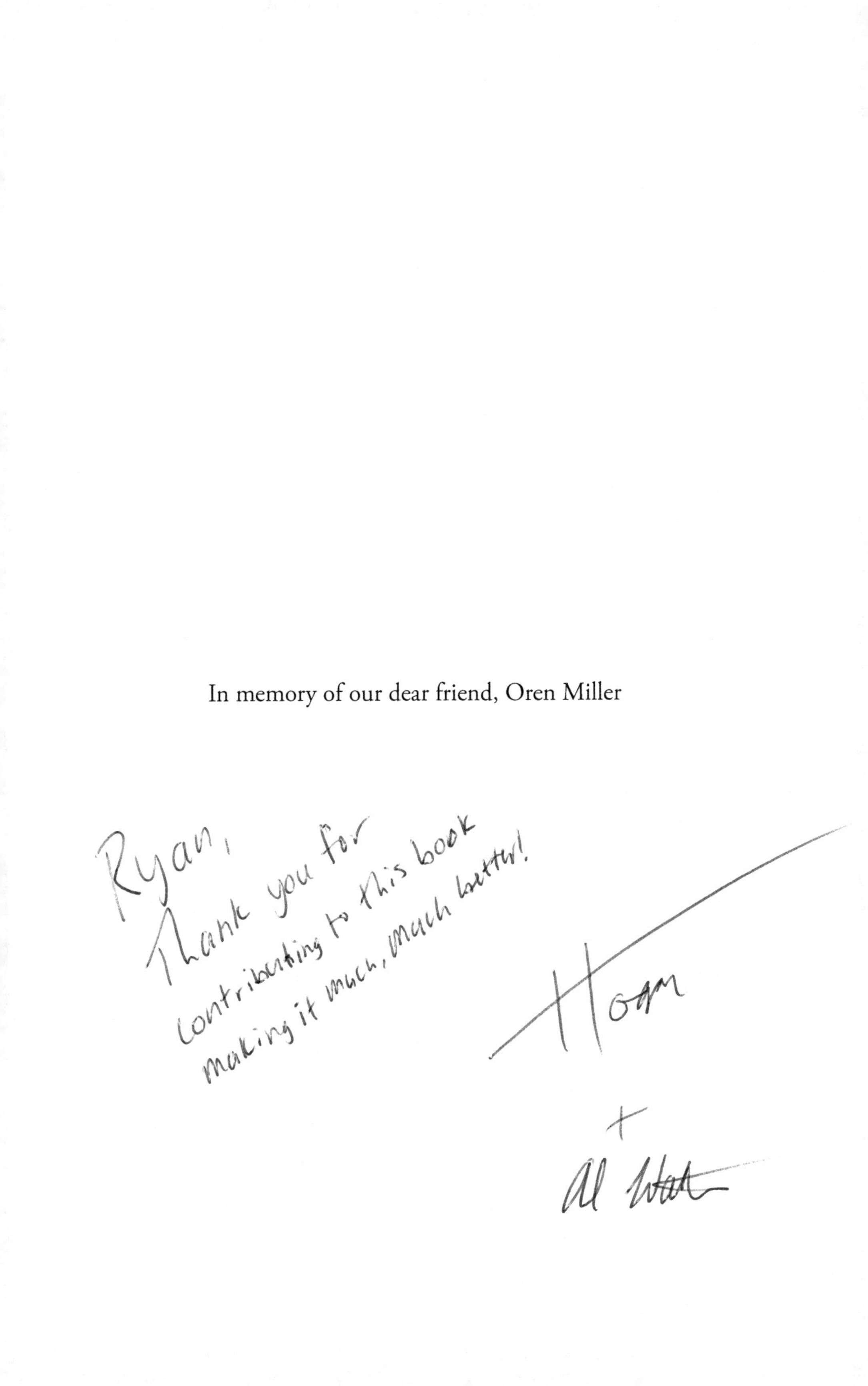

In memory of our dear friend, Oren Miller

Contents

ACKNOWLEDGMENTS

We met Oren Miller, to whom this book is dedicated, in the fall of 2012 at the 17th Annual At-Home Dads Convention in Washington, D.C. We remember him as being a bit shy and having an accent we could not quite place. We remember little else about him from that first meeting.

A few months later, we ran into Oren again at the Houston Airport. We were all attending the Dad 2.0 Summit, a conference for Dad Bloggers, and fate had it that we all arrived from three parts of the country at the same time. We chatted for a while as we waited for our ride to the hotel and then hung out often during the weekend which began a deeper friendship. In the time between the two conferences, Oren, founder of www.BloggerFather.com, had started a Facebook group for dad bloggers, which he quipped was "so crazy, it just might work." We were among the first fifty or so dads he invited to the group.

The Dad Bloggers Facebook Group has since grown to over 1,000 members. It is a great resource for dads to share parenting strategies, advice about blogging, and network with each other. Oren masterfully cultivated the group into a very large brotherhood of fatherhood.

Oren's greatest gift, however, was his writing. We were humbled to have been able to include one of his original stories in our first book, Dads Behaving DADLY: 67 Truths, Tears and Triumphs of Modern Fatherhood. We would have liked to include one of his stories in this book but he ran out of time.

On February 28, 2015, Oren passed away after a nine-month battle with cancer. He left behind two children, a loving wife and a list of friends longer than Santa's Nice List.

We wanted to give this long explanation about our friend because he is one of the most important people in making our two books possible. Most of the contributors to this and our previous book are members of the Dad Bloggers group Oren started. Without this group of brilliant dad writers, and Oren's tremendous support, we would not have been able to assemble such amazing books.

After Oren was diagnosed with cancer, he wrote, "I believe in Heaven on Earth, and I believe it's found anywhere you seek it." It was his way of describing the joys of parenting even when sometimes it doesn't feel like joy at all. We agree.

Many others also deserve recognition in bringing this book to you. Over 130 dads submitted stories to us for this book. They made us laugh and cry. By bravely sharing their vulnerability, we remained committed to bringing this book to life and using their stories to improve the image of fatherhood.

We are grateful to Justin Sachs, CEO of Motivational Press, for continuing to provide unwavering support for this project. We appreciate the outreach by our friend Darren Mattock of Australia, who connected us with our overseas contributors. We are thankful for Brent Almond and John Kinnear, who have taken over the bulk of the administrative duties for the Dad Bloggers Facebook Group. We are also grateful to Brent Almond for designing the cover and Scott Behson, Ph.D. for writing the Foreword.

Hogan would like to further acknowledge Gary Harber and Carrie Taylor for their words of encouragement and support in the publication of the first two books of this series.

Al would like to acknowledge Chad Welch for always being there to listen, his four kids who make him smile everyday, the bitter cold Chicago winter for keeping him inside writing instead of outside redoing the landscaping, God for finally finding a way into his heart and his wife Shirley, who makes each breath he takes sweeter.

FOREWORD

Scott Behson, PhD, Nyack, NY

I recently presented at the Dad 2.0 Summit in San Francisco and was amazed by what I saw. The Summit was attended by writers, bloggers, brands and policy experts, all focused on encouraging involved fatherhood and ensuring the media portrayal of modern fatherhood focuses on it, not as a novelty or a punchline, but rather as an exercise in strength and tenderness, endurance and vulnerability, courage and compassion. All who attended proved it was healthy and normal for a man to be a loving, involved dad while also climbing the corporate ladder, punching the clock to provide for his family, or even removing himself completely from the workforce to be a stay-at-home dad. It was about time we celebrated this.

To me, the Summit represented something of a seismic shift. I mean, can you imagine a conference on this topic a decade ago? Two decades ago? Most dads today live lives that are incongruent with those of their grandfathers. When it comes to masculinity, change has come very quickly, but there has been one persistent barrier: the machismo stereotype.

One of the keynote speakers at the Summit was Dr. Michael Kimmel, perhaps the leading sociologist in the study of masculinity. During his presentation, he showed a New Yorker cartoon on the big screen. It showed two rough and tough-looking cowboys in a saloon, gun belts on their hips and babies in carriers strapped to their chests. One cowboy says to the other "At high noon, I'm taking her to the zoo. How's one thirty?"

Funny, right? But also insightful. Cleverly, the cartoon clarified exactly what made these cowboys manly. It was not their willingness to duel for the sake of honor or pride. Rather, it was that they adjusted their lives to take care of their children.

In a way, we are these cowboys. We have an idea in our heads about what makes someone manly – projecting strength and machismo; John

Wayne, Clint Eastwood, the Rock. But this imagined ideal is out-of-step with what really makes us manly. Taking time out from work to care for our kids – now that is manly. Eschewing destructive macho behavior to ensure we are there for those we love - manly. Working hard at an unfulfilling job to provide for our families - manly. Sharing the load at work and at home equally with our partners - manly. Relating to small children on their level instead of as an unapproachable tower of strength - manly.

In my work, I counsel dads on what they can do to achieve success at work and at home. I also work with employers on how they can be more supportive of working parents in ways where both employers and employees benefit. One of the major obstacles we face is the monolithic, old-school, high-noon, cowboy view of masculinity. But once our society gets past this illusion and sees the world, and manhood, as it really is, that is when progress truly happens.

The "ideal man, ideal worker" is stuck in too many minds and completely out of step with today's society and the modern workplace. Both parents work in 85 percent of two-parent households. Men are no longer the sole breadwinners with at-home wives taking care of the rest. Modern men juggle careers, childcare and housework. Some stay home while their wives take on the role of the breadwinner. Our lives are less gender-role specific than ever. Similarly, the modern workplace no longer emphasizes command and control. Rather, creativity, teamwork, adaptability, judgment and flexibility are the ways to success for modern companies.

One size no longer fits all, either at home or at work. Modern workplaces and, frankly, a whole lot of dads, need to see the reality of manliness in all its variety. That is why I love the work of Hogan and Al, and the whole idea behind Dads Behaving DADLY.

Much like their original book, this volume contains dozens of stories demonstrating masculinity, what it means to be "manly" and, more importantly, what it means to "behave DADLY." These are stories from dads showing compassion and vulnerability, demonstrating true strength and courage. And the best part is that the dads telling their stories throughout the book are us. These aren't fancy-schmantzy professors or consultants like me (although I am a modern dad, too). No pre-eminent sociologists or New Yorker cartoons for that matter. No Brad Pitts or Kobe Bryants. The authors of this book are a cross-section of dads examining their lives and their experiences as fathers, in all its messy reality.

I encourage you to spend some time reading these stories of the amazing and everyday challenges of behaving DADLY, and there is no better time to start than today. I understand that, at high noon, you may be at the zoo with your kids, though. So, how's one-thirty?

Scott Behson, PhD *is Professor of Management at Fairleigh Dickinson University, a busy involved dad, and an overall grateful guy. He is the author of The Working Dad's Survival Guide: How to Succeed at Work and at Home (Motivational Press, 2015) found at www.workingdadsurvivalguide.com, founder of the blog www.fathersworkandfamily.com, has written for Time, Wall Street Journal and Harvard Business Review and has spoken at the White House to advocate for working dads' issues. Scott lives in Nyack, NY with his wife, stage actress Amy Griffin, and son, Nick. Follow him @ScottBehson.*

INTRODUCTION

Al Watts, South Elgin, IL

I was standing at the edge of a cliff in Yellowstone National Park. About 125 feet below lay our then 11-year-old daughter, Anna, on her back, seemingly glued to the near vertical canyon face, black helmet on, arms and legs immobile, one shoe on and one shoe several feet below. Another 150 feet directly below, in the river, was a dark black horse, dead. My wife was kneeling next to our daughter's right side, an EMT on her left. I don't remember breathing.

Anna, her then eight-year-old sister, Macy, and my wife had taken a horse trail ride. Since our other two children were not old enough to ride, I had taken them on a hike in another part of the park. Our girls were excited. These horses would not go in circles on a lead rope. They were going to ride a trail!

When Anna's horse came along the lip of the canyon at an area named Coyote Slide, it took a step to the right for reasons we will never know. It was a fateful step. Beneath that hoof was nothingness. The horse tumbled down into the canyon, our daughter along with it.

It took four hours to extricate her from the canyon. They brought in a rescue helicopter which hoisted her about 1,000 feet into the air to clear the canyon and trees.

As I watched my daughter, secured in a basket that was twisting and turning in the wind, fearing she was paralyzed and possibly dying from internal injuries, one of the EMTs came over and asked if I was all right.

"No I'm not okay!" I screamed, tears gushing down my face. "That's my f***ing daughter!"

Incredibly, she only had minor scrapes and bruises. No internal injuries. No paralysis. Within a week, she had completely recovered and was running, jumping, swimming and being her sassy self.

It took longer for me to stop crying. Much longer.

What helped me recover was sharing my story. I posted it on Facebook. I called several friends who listened in stunned silence as I tearfully retold the story. I stood in front of seventy other dads at the Annual At-Home Dads Convention in Denver, CO a few months after the accident and told them the story. Many of the dads, some who had never met me before, cried openly along with me.

We are living in the first generation in which men are realizing the definition of masculinity needs an upgrade. Our society has taught men we are supposed to be tough and stoic. Through the good and bad, and sometimes ugly experiences from our own fathers, today's dads are recognizing masculinity is much broader and includes hands-on involvement with their children, vulnerability and compassion.

Hogan and I have discovered, through sharing our experiences - our truths, tears and triumphs - and encouraging other dads to do the same, helps dads heal, gives dads the confidence to be better partners and parents and allows them to connect with their children on a deeper level. Through our years of experience as fathers and advocates for involved fatherhood, as leaders of dad clubs, the National At-Home Dad Network and appearances on hundreds of TV, radio and print interviews, we know dads need a safe place to be emotionally vulnerable.

And that is why we compiled this series.

The stories we tell, as dads, free us from the shackles of outdated masculinity. You have, or will, experience something similar to every single story in this book. You will discover empathy for the joys and heartaches the dads share in their stories. It will affirm what you know in your heart to be true about yourself and we hope it inspires you to share your stories, allowing you to be emotionally vulnerable, providing you with a deeper connection to your children.

Our first book accomplished this for moms and dads all over the world. James H. wrote on his five-star review of our book on amazon.com, "There are several, excellent examples, in this book, of the enlightened moments as well as the darker parts. The heartbreak, the heart feels and the hilarity."

Another reviewer wrote, "I cried. I laughed. I related." Christopher Bakker found me on Facebook and wrote, "Your book made me teary eyed on the CTA Brown line in Chicago."

You will experience much the same emotions with our second edition. The pain and joy of our fathers was an important aspect of modern fatherhood we chose to explore in this book and made it the first section. In subsequent sections, we have dads describing the heartache associated with the loss from a miscarriage, the frustrating uncertainty of the NICU, the near-death experiences from accidents. We also have dads who show how they parent uniquely as men, how dads deal with anxiety and depression, how the things dads teach their children make them swell with pride and how, sometimes, parenting is just darn right hilarious.

The dads in this book provide you with a glimpse into what modern fatherhood is like for most families. We expect, in some way, you will be able to relate to each dad's story. Our goal is for you to feel what they feel and, hopefully, recognize those feelings within yourself.

The stories contained here display the depth of vulnerability men are capable of as fathers. We believe it is affirming and inspirational. And, DADLY.

PART ONE
OUR FATHERS

"My own father walked out when I was two, and he didn't look back for years. When he eventually did, the damage was already done and it would take twenty-six years for my wounds to heal, something that only came with the birth of my first child."

- *Benjamin Pratt, Armidale, NSW, Australia*

SHOULDERS

Eric Boyette, Tampa, FL

I stand here in front of him as he sits in the swing, enjoying the soft breeze of the mid-September afternoon. He is blissfully unaware I'm blocking the blinding rays from his eyes with my shadow. My shoulders are wide enough to eclipse the sun and allow him to enjoy the last drops of a cool fall day, unperturbed by the glaring orange disc behind me. At a year and a half, his biggest problem at the moment is retrieving the last dried strawberry from the bag he clutches in his tiny hands. I know how high I can push without frightening him and I keep him moving with the slow, steady consistency of a pendulum easily metered by the repetitious whine of metal on metal, interrupted only by the drone of traffic. He has no fear of the unknown, and therefore, no appreciation for the safety I provide. His blue eyes gleam like sapphires as he laughs and squeals. I shoulder the weight of his safety as he learns to keep himself from harm. When we leave the park, he'll ride the same shoulders and we'll stroll home, enjoying the city's sounds, sights and smells in the twilight of the day and the season.

Any mortal in their right mind would be terrified to be hoisted three times their own height atop a giant, but he knows nothing of fear. I have trouble teaching him actions have consequences, not wanting to diminish his intrepid spirit. How do I teach him without scaring him? I want him to believe the slide continues curving away beyond his sight. I want him to have faith the thrill is worth a moment of uncertainty. I don't want my warnings of caution to water the seeds of doubt. He's already assembling a respectable collection of bruises on his shins and bumps on his head, but I know the deepest cuts are years in the distance. I see them coming, as inevitable as the end of this afternoon. No need to mention them, we'll have plenty of time for that. I have faith in the time. Time won't let me down.

Will it?

My hope as a father is to remedy all that ails my children. To protect them at all times from all dangers, both real and perceived, while teaching them to do the same for themselves along the way. There will be time for that, the shadows will grow much longer before mine fades to black. The truth is, I think I'm doing okay at this dad thing. I had some good teachers; I stand on the shoulders of giants.

My dad is a great father, as was his. I rode on his shoulders when I was my son's age. I enjoyed their shade when I was swinging, and I cried into them when life seemed unfair. My father taught me how to stand on his shoulders literally, then, with his love and support, I learned the far more difficult task of standing on those shoulders figuratively.

It is not the piggyback rides along Myrtle Beach that come to mind when I think of those shoulders, but the times they carried me through the rough patches of my life. I was blissfully unaware of his diligent protection when I was younger. I had little experience with fear. Security was a gift I didn't know I had been given. My father was there when a "big kid" pushed me off a big wheel. He was there when I struggled with self-esteem in junior high and he taught me not to define myself with the expectations and judgments of others. When a bully attacked me on the bus for defending my sister, he was there to stand up for me when I was nearly suspended. My father taught me about fairness and courage. His ideas of justice were a constant theme in my childhood, running deep, like a vein of iron through a mountain range. My dad was there when I didn't make the grade and when I did. He was there as loved ones left this world, there when I struggled in college and there when I searched for a career. He did not tell me where to go or what to do, and no matter where I turned, his shadow always danced ahead even when he was not physically present. My father was there to remind me that my path was my own, that no one would or should prepare it for me. He was there when I fell in and out of love, there when I made bad decisions, there when I succeeded at work, there when I lost a good job, and there when I married my wife. He's been there following the birth of each of my children; always wanting to show support while not wanting to be in the way, always giving me the space to live and experience life in my own way. There are times these days when my father's shadow isn't as clear to me and we don't talk as often as we should (a shared fault), but when I look a little closer, I can usually see his silhouette against the hard sun of life. His shadow hides the danger, and in doing so, obscures it's own presence. I know when the day comes and the sun sets on my father, the absence of that cool shade will become shockingly clear ... blindingly so. I'll squint at the unforgiving sun. I'll hide my eyes in my hands and I'll weep. Afterwards, I suspect I will spend years realizing the full myriad of ways he protected, supported and encouraged me. I stand on the shoulders of my dad, as he did on his.

As I continue down the path of fatherhood, I enjoy the satisfaction of knowing my shadow will grow longer and provide respite from the cruel elements for those I love the most. I don't say that out of pride for myself, but out of pride in all of us. It gives me a peaceful, reassuring feeling to know my helpless little boy will one day cast an epic shadow indeed. He will stand against the sun, the wind and the rain. A solid rock to anchor those who love him and to stand against any who would do them harm.

The amazing thing is how much growth my children have precipitated within me as well. That thought makes me happy as I try to conceptualize how my father grew with me. In our family, we are sustaining each other and laying the foundation for the future with every laugh and every tear. Now, as our shadows lengthen, we walk home with the sun at our backs and my son on my shoulders. I have to wonder whose shadow stretches ahead of us leading us home.

__Eric Boyette__ is father of two, currently living in the Tampa Bay area. He pursued his dream of being a writer during his time as an at-home father. He has written for the Huffington Post, Good Men Project, National At-Home Dad Network and has his own blog, DadOnTheRun.com. While still writing, Eric is now the Director of Special Investigations with an international investigative firm, meaning his kids have no chance during a game of hide-and-seek, but he claims to still be unable to find the remote. Two of his stories also appeared in Dads Behaving Dadly: 67 Truths, Tears and Triumphs of Modern Fatherhood *under the pseudonym Eric Jefferson.*

REVERSE THE CURSE

Vincent Fitzgerald MSW LSW, Jersey City, NJ

Down two runs with two outs and the bases loaded in the final inning, my 11-year-old son stepped up to home plate. The minute he dug his cleats into the moist dirt, his "Mudville" moment weighed on me. There were two possible outcomes. He would be the last out, or his team's hero. I peered through the chain-link fence separating me from the batter's box in which Aedan stood, knees bent, wagging bat pointed skyward.

I gripped the links with clawed hands, creating fresh creases in my fingers. Aedan locked eyes with the diminutive opposing pitcher while I fixed my gaze on him, praying he wouldn't freeze. We lived 47 miles from each other, yet the distance between us on the field seemed greater. I wanted to be in the box with him, if only to whisper to him that making the final out was acceptable, but allowing fear to fasten his bat to his shoulder was a failure he might one day regret.

This was a moment custodial dads might take for granted relative to the daily minutiae experienced by intact families. Divorce fractured our family and rendered me bereft of good night kisses, seeing my son off to school, and looking into his eyes as he recounted his day. As a dad from a distance, this moment was a treasure, one that held a place in my mental trophy case.

Flip flopping between enjoyment and nervousness, an infantry of melancholic memories of my brief little league experience invaded my thoughts. At a time when fences separated me from the dads of other kids, apathy separated me from mine. I imagined pretend cheers from my father, whose absence shredded my confidence and fractured my ego. It was my misfortune that early morning games started too soon after last call.

While I struggled on the field, he slept under blankets, trapping the stench of the previous night's excesses only five blocks from my field of failure. Unsupported, I compiled one hit in a two-season career truncated by futility. In the outfield, I prayed the ball never found me. My coaches knew it and exiled me to right field, or little league Siberia. At the plate, my bat lay leaden on my shoulder, which resulted in walks or strikeouts. I would mope back toward disappointed teammates, dragging my bat, leaving a trail in the dirt behind me.

My grandfather's prioritizing of alcohol and women over his sons cursed my father who, in turn, visited that curse upon me. Had I carried on in the same manner as past generations, I would have placed my son, and maybe one day his son, at risk. I knew I was not the most attentive of fathers when I lived with my family. My mistakes made it obvious I was on the same path. I was younger then, self-absorbed, but age and the possibility of continuing the curse beseeched me to succeed in divorce where I had failed in marriage.

Aedan worked the count to two balls and two strikes. Contrary to my stationary at bats, the swings resulting in two strikes were frenzied activity. I muted cheers, offering a raised thumb when he glanced my way, assuring him I was present in success, or otherwise, sparing him the despair of desertion that hindered me when I looked to be lifted by my father's glance. As long as Aedan tried, I assured him there would be no failure.

After my on-field woes, I fantasized about my dad walking me to our beige Chevy; arm around me, offering a Life Saver to quell my disappointment the way Mr. Cunningham once did for Richie after a missed free throw on Happy Days. Instead, I walked home with teammates, listening to them brag about their highlights while I stayed silent. My father never asked about my games. It was welcomed apathy considering my dearth of successful moments.

With the count now full, I bit my tongue to keep silent, wary of being a distraction. On the sixth pitch, Aedan swung with a force that shifted his helmet, lining the ball inside the third base line. My explosive cheer startled other parents, but excitement deflected my embarrassment. Now hanging from the fence like a chimp in a zoo cage, I watched as a wide-eyed Aedan raced toward first base, raising dirt clouds with each stride as runners on third and second raced toward home. Every detail became a Polaroid in my memory. While standing on the bag, Aedan looked my way. I touched my heart with my index finger and pointed it at him, his cherub face smiling back.

Just after the winning run crossed home plate, I ignored protocol, storming the field and hugging Aedan as jubilant teammates pushed through me for a high five or to tap his helmet. When the excitement waned and the crowd disbursed, we walked to our car, bound at the hip. My arm was wrapped tightly around him, laying as heavy on his shoulder as my bat used to lay on mine. I peppered Aedan with questions about his hit. "How does it feel to be the hero?" "Did you feel the vibration of the bat up your arms?" He couldn't spit out his answers fast enough before the next question burst from my mouth.

Having found the ball laying at home plate, I took it, knowing full well it would be the most valuable piece of sports memorabilia I would ever own. I placed it in my glove compartment where it remains. If ever Aedan doubts himself, I can show him the ball. When I feel distance diminish my role as Aedan's dad, the ball reminds me of my necessity in his life.

After two abject years in little league, I never again played an organized sport, paralyzed by a biting fear of public failure. My son, however, is not afraid to try, nor is he afraid to fail. It is success in itself, and it eclipses my achievements the way loving dads hope sons do. I look forward to the day he gets to watch his own bat-wagging child, untainted by melancholic memories.

I've often wallowed in self-pity whenever I reminisced about those formative years, during which I was deprived of support from my father. But, as I've aged, I have put my pity in its rightful place, square on the sloping shoulders of my father. His support may not have guaranteed my success as an athlete, but it could have injected me with confidence, and would have had a profound impact on me. He could have been first to reverse the curse. Instead, he is the lone mourner at an eternal wake for dead opportunities.

Vincent Fitzgerald MSW LSW, *born and raised in Jersey City, is currently a psychotherapist for the Nutley Family Service Bureau. He works with individuals, couples, and families, hoping to keep them intact during times of struggle. He has a 17-year-old daughter, Emily, and 12-year-old son, Aedan. As a divorced dad, he tries his best to do a better job than his father, remaining active in the lives of his kids.*

DAD IN TRAINING

Kevin Barske, Winnipeg, MB, Canada

Before we had kids of our own, I never really had much contact with babies (or young children for that matter). I have a brother who is four years younger and a couple of younger cousins but that is the extent of it. So, when my wife Heather became pregnant with our first, I had virtually no idea what to expect. Like many new parents, I was terrified by the thought of being responsible for someone other than myself. All kinds of doubts buzzed through my head. Would I be worthy of this precious young life? What kind of dad would I be? Would I make a good role model? Would I be able to successfully raise this child to be a kind and caring human being? As this violent torrent of thoughts cascaded through my mind, I began to reflect upon my experience as a child and my relationship with my father.

I started to think about all the times my dad was there for my brother and I. Don't get me wrong, my mom was always there for us too (she was a stay-at-home mom until we were in school), but my relationship with my dad was the benchmark I used for how to be a good dad. And to be honest, he set the bar pretty high. He worked full-time as a teacher but always made time for us. He taught us how to box and how to shoot a wrist shot in hockey. He taught us how to drive a car and how not to light a gas-powered potato gun. He let us "help" him make the bed by having us lay perfectly still while he fluffed the sheets gently over us like a parachute.

After flipping through the memory vault of my dad, a thought occurred to me. He needed to know how I felt. I reached for the phone and dialed that well-known number.

"Hello?" came the familiar voice of my dad.

I suddenly burst into tears, as the flood of great memories washed over me. I couldn't speak, I was so overcome with emotion. My dad was starting to get worried, hearing nothing but blubbering over the line.

"Kev?" he asked. "Is everything OK?"

Still unable to speak, I could hear the fear working it's way into my dad's normally steady voice. "Did something happen to the baby?"

"No" I managed to squeak.

"Did something happen to Heather?"

Another squeak. "No."

I needed to pull myself together before I gave my dad a heart attack. I took a few deep breaths, composing myself long enough to tell my Dad what I wanted him to hear.

"Heather and the baby are fine," I said. "I was just thinking about what a great dad you are and I wanted to make sure you knew that. One day, I hope I am as good a dad as you are."

My dad has never been overly emotional (in public at least) and I could probably count on one hand the number of times I've ever heard him cry, but that day, another finger was added to the tally.

"Thank you, Kev," he finally managed.

"No dad. Thank you. You are an amazing dad and I just wanted to let you know how I feel."

After writing the initial draft of this story, I emailed a copy to my dad to make sure he was okay with me sharing it. As it turns out, he was more than okay with it. After he read the first draft he replied to my email with the following: "You have no idea how much this 'Dad story' means to me. It is definitely one of the high points of my entire life and something which I will always treasure."

Too often in life we take for granted those who matter most to us. Unfortunately, it is often once these people are no longer with us when we realize we did not express our feelings towards them. By then, it is too late. We need to take ownership of our feelings and tell the special people in our lives what they mean to us. Although they probably have an idea based on how we treat them, it might just make their day to actually hear those words out loud or to see them written on a screen.

As cliché as this may sound, I have loved my dad my whole life. However, I don't think he truly grasped the depth of my love for him until he read this story. I felt a great sense of relief, knowing what an impact my words had on my dad. It also makes me feel good knowing I shared my feelings with him while he was still able to appreciate them.

When I decided to share this story, I did it out of love. I wrote it for my dad. I did not expect anything from him in return, but being the man he is, he returned the favor. At the end of his return email to me, he wrote, "I want you to know that I have often thought as I watch you with Claire and Logan...that you have turned out to be a far better father than I ever was."

Upon reflection, it turns out, I've been a dad in training my whole life without realizing it. I was more than ready for the role, thanks to my dad.

***Kevin Barske**, is a stay-at-home dad to a six-year-old girl and a three-year-old boy and loving husband to his wife, Heather. Before children, he worked as an MRI Technologist at a local sports medicine clinic. In his occasional free time, he studies photography and permaculture. In 2013 he co-founded the Winnipeg Dads Group (www.winnipegdads.com). Being a dad is the best job he has ever had.*

THE PRESENCE OF ABSENCE

Jameson Mercier, Plantation, FL

I remember badly wanting a dog. I was going to name him Mickey. My mother was not having it. I begged. I pleaded. My mom didn't budge. One day, my father walked into the house after a long day of work and told me he had something for me in his cab. I went out to his cab, squished my face against the passenger window and peered inside, but I didn't see anything. I opened the door and there, on the floorboard, was Mickey. Filled with the greatest joy I had yet experienced, I grabbed him and rushed into the house. It was the last gift I received from my father.

Most kids grow up with a lot of memories of their fathers. I only have a few. What I know of my father was that he was an immigrant from Haiti and he drove a taxi. Those who knew him, tell me my father was the type of guy who liked to live life to the fullest. Although he was a hustler and a hard worker, he made sure to enjoy the fruits of his labor. He had fun and always tried to make other people happy, especially his kids. I don't remember him being someone who would have long and deep conversations, but he seemed to be available when you needed him.

I looked up to him, like most sons look up to their fathers. Once in the driveway of our family home, I remember telling him I wanted to be just like him when I grew up. What he said next stayed with me for the rest of my life. He immediately became very upset. He looked me straight in the eye and yelled, "Never say that again!" I was shocked, confused and upset. I did not understand it then, at eight years old, but it became clearer as I grew older: my father wanted me to do better than him.

Like many children of color in America, I did not grow up with my father. Unlike many of those kids, it was not because he was incarcerated or absent. I was born in Haiti during an era of massive anti-government demonstrations, Duvalier (Baby Doc) and the Tonton Macoute. Many

Haitians at the time left Haiti in search of a better life, including my mother and father. They were unable to take me, only two years old at the time, on the treacherous journey to the United States. I was left behind in the care of extended family. It would be five years before they could afford to bring me to the U.S. Unfortunately, my father would pass away two years later. I didn't get to know him as well as I would have liked.

I remember being very angry after he died, but not sure why. I used to get into fights simply because I had nothing else to do. There were times my mother and I got into disagreements. In those moments, I remember wishing my father were still around. Perhaps he would understand. No one else did.

Eventually, I got myself on to the straight and narrow path. I took my dad's advice and tried to better myself. I went to college, found a smart and beautiful woman to marry and became a licensed therapist.

When my wife and I began talking about having children, I was filled with doubt about my ability to be a good dad. I questioned how I was going to be a good father when I grew up, mostly, without one. The thought of the responsibility was overwhelming and terrifying. It filled me with anxiety because I thought I had no role model or guide.

As I thought more about becoming a father, I began to realize how much I had learned from my dad. His absence taught me a lot, especially about myself. Although he left Haiti to set up a better life for us, he left a hole in our relationship that never had time to close. I observed how his absence changed my mom. I was keenly aware of the immense void one feels when growing up without a father. Families, I learned, were stronger together.

I realized his absence was why I would bypass job opportunities because it would not be possible to bring my family with me. His absence was why I made sure to spend as much time with my wife as I could. His absence was why I decided the best thing I could do for my kids was to be involved in their lives as much as possible: taking them to the park, teaching them to drive, interrogating my daughters' boyfriends, guiding my son into manhood, and embarrassing them in public.

Seven years ago, the thought of being a dad terrified me. Today, I'm very comfortable in my role as my children's father. The absence of my father taught me to be present. I have been able to do better than him, just as he told me to. And I'm certain my dad would be proud of me.

***Jameson Mercier** is a dad to three children, Asrielle, six, Tamar, four, and Jaeson, two, and husband to his lovely wife Herdyne. Jameson is a Licensed Clinical Social Worker in private practice. He is completing his doctorate degree in Marriage and Family Therapy at Nova Southeastern University. His research focuses on fathers as primary caregivers. He is also an adjunct professor of social work at Barry University, and Nova Southeastern University. Jameson and his family live in Fort Lauderdale, Florida. One of his stories also appeared in* Dads Behaving Dadly: 67 Truths, Tears and Triumphs of Modern Fatherhood.

I MISSED HIM

Hogan Hilling, Crestline, CA

I missed not having a dad in my life.

My mom never talked about him. All I knew was that his name was Henk and that my mom and Henk divorced after I turned two.

In school, I dreaded the question teachers and kids asked, "What does your dad do?"

With a crushed heart, I would reply, "I don't have a dad."

As a child, I didn't know how to share the pain of not having a dad or who to share it with. I struggled with my identity and with the question of why I was one of the few children without a dad in his life. Mostly, I really, really missed my dad.

The middle and high school years were extremely difficult because I had no dad to guide me into manhood. I questioned my existence, struggled with self-esteem and had a hard time trusting people. My rage and anger at Henk for robbing me of life without a dad also grew.

Why did he leave? How could he leave? If he is still alive, why didn't he come back?

By the time I graduated high school, the pain dwindled into acceptance but never disappeared. Although I surrendered to the reality I would never meet my dad, I hung on to a glimmer of hope for a reunion with him. If it did happen, I wondered how I would react.

In 1983, twenty-six years after my parents divorced, fate gave me an opportunity to answer my question. It began with a phone call from my brother.

My brother told me about how he had introduced himself to a man while on a visit to San Francisco. The gentleman said he knew another man with the last name Hilling. That man turned out to be our dad's brother, Theo. My brother got his number and I called Theo who put me in contact with my dad, who was living in Brazil!

My reunion with Henk began with a letter, followed by a phone call and eventually a flight to Brazil.

At the time I owned a business. I closed it and committed to spending time with Henk and his new family for six months. This was a once in a lifetime opportunity. I didn't want to pass it up even if it meant losing my business.

Father and child reunions after so many years are rare. When it does occur, it is difficult for father and child to bury the hatchet and renew their relationship. I decided to let bygones be bygones and gave Henk a clean slate. No animosity. No judgment. No assumptions. No expectations. No drama.

During the first five months there weren't many opportunities for a one-on-one chat with Henk who had a full-time job and family responsibilities.

Much of my time was spent bonding with Henk's wife, Claudette, and children Heady, Dewi and Anna Lisa. In addition to the good fortune of my reunion with Henk, his new family embraced me with open arms. Claudette treated me like her biological son and Henk's daughters treated me like their biological big brother. I felt so lucky to have finally become part of a real family.

My time with Henk and his family proved to be more than just a reunion of father and son. As I observed Henk's mannerisms and interaction with his family, I began to develop a greater understanding of who I was. I recognized qualities, characteristics, and personality traits as well as shortcomings Henk and I had in common. My time with Henk and his family turned out to be very therapeutic.

One of Henk's traits that impressed me was his pride. Henk took great pride in every aspect of his role as a loving, passionate, dedicated, involved husband and father. There was no doubt Henk loved his family. He demonstrated it every day with public displays of affection.

Henk also took great pride in his job as draftsman for one of Brazil's largest energy companies. On my lunch visits to his office, I met many co-workers who shared how much they resected and admired Henk.

I felt proud to call him my dad.

Henk's pride for his work is what led to the defining moment of our reunion. He invited me to visit one of the power plants he helped design, which was located in the middle of the Brazilian jungle. During the drive, we had alone time to share more of our personal stories of life without each other.

Three hours into the drive, Henk pulled to the side of the two-lane road near a creek surrounded by miles of banana trees. He turned off the engine and finally shared his side of the story.

"After your mother asked for the divorce, we went our separate ways. I stayed in Brazil and she moved to the Netherlands with you and your brother. I was devastated. I tried many times to contact you through letters but I never received a reply. I lost track of time and didn't know your whereabouts. Sometimes I feel I didn't try hard enough to find you and your brother. I'm sorry that I wasn't there for you. I hope you will forgive me."

As I listened to the pain in Henk's voice, the many why's I had asked about Henk no longer mattered. While I wallowed in my pain of life without a father, I never thought about the agony of my dad's life without a son. I realized Henk had missed me more than I had missed him.

"Dad, I accept your apology but it is unnecessary. I'm so grateful we met and I love you!" I told him.

Later that day I made a pact with myself. If I ever became a dad, I would do whatever it took to be a hands-on, involved dad for two reasons. One reason was an unselfish one. I would not want my children to experience the life I had without a father. The second was a selfish one. I would never want to experience the emotional pain Henk endured in a life without all of his children.

Today, I'm proud to have fulfilled my pact as a father to three boys, who are now adults.

Henk passed away in 1995. Although my relationship with him only lasted twelve years, I have many fond father/son memories I still cherish today.

But I still miss him.

***Hogan Hilling** is a dad, motivational speaker and award-winning author of five parenting books. As a well-respected voice on involved fatherhood, Hogan has conducted hundreds of seminars for moms and dads, appeared on Oprah, The Story of Fathers & Sons Documentary, ABC's Story of Fathers and Sons, NBC's The Other Half and Unsung Heroes and has received the California Courage to Care Award. Follow him @TheDadGuru.*

DAD BROKE

Rob Azevedo, Manchester, NH

When my Dad died four years ago he was broke, both financially and emotionally.

Cancer killed him at 70 but he had been dad broke for nearly twenty years.

I still can't find the guts to delete his number from my cellphone. We were tight, so much alike, and yet so different. We were both heavy tempered, both self-conscious, both fueled by short attention spans and a dire need to be heard, someway, somehow. Still, when you're watching a parent die, or anyone you love die, the horror is all you feel. Who cares about the past when your old man's arm is being cut off to slow the cancer down? The last thing I was thinking about while I watched him die for a year was if we had enough games of catch in the front yard when I was a kid.

Of course, maybe that was because I wasn't even allowed to play on the front lawn. "Landscapers only!" my dad used to yell at me.

When we learned my father had virtually nothing left to his name in the form of property or finances when he died, we were shocked. We knew he wasn't well off anymore. We just didn't know he was busted.

The 1980's were a wonderful time to make money, if you didn't mind the hustle. My dad hustled as an insurance salesman. He worked his way off a furniture truck to become a ritzy country-club card carrier with a booming financial business outside Boston. My father drove a sports car, bought a big brick house, smoked a lot of butts, and read a lot of books. By age 50 he was a success!

Also, my dad could be a difficult man. He had few friends, probably a good many lovers, a pretty bad marriage and four solid kids (for the most part). He had the ability to fly off the handle, to belittle, love, aggravate, instigate and succeed.

Then, after he turned 50, he got sick of being a success. He became disappointed in his life, disinterested in his career and became generally bored. That's when he took up acting. His new passion became another reason for me to sit back and love him more. Here was a guy I would see, night after night, sitting on the couch reading an Agatha Christie classic. One day he came home, announcing he was done selling insurance. He was going to put all his energies into acting. All those characters in the hundreds of books he read made him want to matter.

The next thing I knew, we were going into Harvard Square to see him perform in a play about a washed up prizefighter in some small church theatre. He was awesomely rough, but awesome! My dad, up there on stage, balls out, laying the smack down on all that wordage, memorized down to the nuts.

It was a favorite moment of mine with him.

If there was one thing about my relationship with my father I wish was better was that we weren't close enough. We were close. I could lean on him, but there would be a price to pay, so lots of times I didn't. Maybe there should be a price to pay for tough love. Maybe his toughness made me a tender father. Maybe I saw the benefits of having a hard ass father and decided, "Okay, I've seen that game played. Now, I'm going to do it different when I have a kid. See how that goes."

I'm fine with that. Variety far outweighs repetition.

My favorite time with my dad was definitely when I was in my late 20's. He liked my friends more than he did his own generation. To him, people his age were boring, dead in the eyes, yammering on about the same sicknesses. When he hung out with us, I think he was able to reveal himself more. He liked to carry a room, and he did. He liked to smoke butts, and he did. He liked to talk about movies and books and babes. He liked a whole lot of stuff. Then he didn't. He stopped carrying a room, just infecting it at times, with his ill manners and testiness. He stopped acting, calling, or caring, because he couldn't get out of his own head.

And then he got broke.

Prophetic in hiding his financial demise, out of pride and shame, my father found himself so underwater that he stopped fighting the current. Like so many his age, he was more broke than anyone knew. He retired too early at 53. He stopped hustling and dreamed way too big. With earnings out of the equation, every buck he borrowed and spent led him deeper into the abyss.

Had we, his children, an inkling he was drowning in something other than the disease, we would have helped. But the Christmas cards with cash inside arrived each year for the grandkids. Weddings and dinners were paid for, college educations were funded, and credit was extended. He refused to let on.

I hold none of this against my father. He was no street urchin, thumbing for nickels on a cold, dark winter's night. He was a survivor. If he decided to spend his fortune, it was his right to do so. Not a nickel of his money came easy. He was a salesman, but not a people person. He was a dad, but not terribly dadly. He was a provider, but never let you forget how good we had it. He was real, maybe too real.

But he was my father. And I loved him.

***Rob Azevedo**, from Manchester, NH, is married with two children. He is a writer, a short filmmaker and a radio host on WNHN out of Concord NH. His writings have been featured in newspapers and magazines for the past 20 years. He is also the "music man" for the Concord Monitor and can be reached at onemanmanch@gmail.com.*

SAYING "I LOVE YOU"

John Engel, Florence, MA

Finally, it's 8 p.m.

The pre-supper meltdowns, dinner-table antics, rambunctious post-dinner play, bath time, pajamas, teeth brushing and story time have come to an end, at least for today. The kids are finally in bed. The house is nearly silent. My wife Lori heads to the bathroom for a steamy shower and I am off to the computer to read my email.

In my inbox is a message from my father. This is probably the fourth or fifth time he has sent me an email.

No one has ever accused my father of being an early-adopter. He greets new products, gadgets and trendy ways of doing things with great suspicion.

He has never owned a computer. Never will. My old-school, self-reliant and frugal father, who ardently believes that public schools and libraries are unnecessary burdens on his inflated property tax bill is, nevertheless, a regular at the local public library computer station.

The email was one of those electronic chain letters with a long list of positive, heart-warming comments ending with a passionate plea that you forward it to everyone you ever knew and cared about, so you can be rewarded with evidence of your extensive network of friends and family when it circles back to you.

If it had been from anyone else, I would have hit "delete" without reading more than the subject line. My father's note was brief: "I thought you would like this and might use some in your column." The letter included 32 statements attributed to the late Andy Rooney, each beginning with the words, "I've learned … "

One of the lessons: "I've learned … that I wish I could have told my Dad that I love him one more time before he passed away."

My throat knotted. In recent years, my father and I have mumbled "I love you" to each other a few times. The most recent occasion was when I dropped him off at the airport following a five-day visit with our family. Like a young boy preparing to jump off the high-dive platform, I had to work up the courage to speak those three words.

The list of mothers and daughters, as well as mothers and sons, who routinely say "I love you" to each other is much longer than the list of fathers and sons who do the same. As a child, like many of my peers, I was not accustomed to hearing those words from my father. I have no doubt those words were even less familiar to my father and his peers.

One lesson fatherhood has taught me is, words aside, fathers love their children just as much as mothers do. Among my favorite baby photos is a black-and-white image of my father, fast asleep in a recliner, with me dozing on his chest.

During his recent visit I did not hear him say "I love you" to his grandchildren, two-year-old Adam and five-year-old Zoe. But in the middle of the night, I found him kneeling at my son's bedside, despite a replaced hip and an arthritic knee, whispering reassurances when Adam cried because of a nightmare.

Ready to join Lori for pillow talk about the day, I powered down the computer and shut off the lights. I crouched next to Adam's bed, watching the rhythm of his body as he inhaled and exhaled, and said, "I love you, little buddy." Then I snuggled alongside Zoe, brushing back the wisps of hair that covered her eyes, and said, "I love you, sweetie."

As I headed to bed, I wondered what sweet things my father had whispered to me while I was sleeping.

***John Engel** is a father, husband, organizational consultant and writer. He is Director of The Fatherhood Journey, with a mission to promote private and public conversations about fatherhood. His monthly column, 'The Fatherhood Journey,' runs in the Daily Hampshire Gazette and is available at www.fatherhoodjourney.com. John is also Coordinator of the Healthy Men and Boys Network of Western Massachusetts, which can be viewed at www.hmbnetwork.org.*

DESPITE AND BECAUSE OF HIM

Christopher Persley, New York, NY

For the first time in eleven years, I read the novel, Things Fall Apart by Chinua Achebe. As an English teacher, I honestly feel each time you read a book you see different things. I have become a husband and father since I last read it, and I recognized things in the characters and story I had not appreciated before. The protagonist, Okonkwo, is not the most liked character. He is a poor father at best, due in large part to his relationship with his father who is not much of a role model. Everything Okonkwo does is in response to his father's failures and ineptitude. I can relate to Okonkwo. My father was out of my life by age five. I had one conversation with him on the phone at age twelve and only reconnected with him a few years ago after twenty-five years of absence.

Although we have been working on creating a relationship, that's a long time without talking to a parent. Honestly, I didn't know what he would sound or look like after twenty-five years. Most of my life I viewed him as a deadbeat, the guy who left me. My only memories of him were negative. He gave me cheap toys for Christmas that would break before New Year's. He would pick me up to spend time with me only to leave me with family members or random people so he could do something else. He set the bar pretty low for fatherhood.

Who were the fathers with a parenting style I could model? Maybe Heathcliff Huxtable, who everyone wished was their father, giving his kids zerberts or winter time BBQ's? Maybe Chris Gardner of The Pursuit of Happyness, whose sole motivation was the survival of his son at all costs, while overcoming poor business decisions and homelessness.

I did not lack male role models, though. There were certainly some in my middle school years, in particular, one of the few men of color I had as a teacher. I remember talking with him often, knowing he truly was looking out for me. He knew I was challenged by being one of a handful of black boys at the school. He even took me to purchase my first pair of track shoes. As close as I was to my mother, I was grateful to have this connection with a black man.

Thankfully, my mother was beyond competent. Through her influence and my utter disgust for my father, I began to behave and perform in ways that would not only make my mother proud, but I hoped would also make my father sad. My academic success in independent schools and degrees from two great universities, my sports prowess, my career in education, the pride I took in being a sensitive and thoughtful man, are connected to my desire to not be like my father. I was mad at him for abandoning me. I wanted to show him what he had missed. I wanted him to know I was able to thrive without him. I wanted him to regret his decision to leave. I wanted to distance myself so far from him that I desperately wanted to change my middle name, which is his first name.

Recently, however, I have come to the conclusion that I am the man I am today despite my father AND because of him. My father, unwittingly, motivated me. His failures as a parent inspired me to be a strong parent. When my daughter was born and I was able to hold her, making her existence so much more real, I could not imagine being absent for one second. No way would I be unreliable or a negative influence in her life.

When it comes down to it, my mother's efforts need to be commended. If she wasn't so strong, smart, and thoughtful, I would not have been able to understand the magnitude of my successes. For that, and so much else, I am happy to call her Mom, and I give her my sincere thanks. My "relationship" with my father is certainly a reason why I am a stay-at-home dad. I want my daughter to have a lasting and strong bond with her father. So thank you, Dad, for allowing me to create my own model of fatherhood, one that works for my family. Because of you, I am straight killin' this fatherhood thing.

Christopher Persley *is an at-home father living in New York City with his wife and three-year-old daughter. He writes at his blog, www.thebrowngothamite.com. In addition, Christopher is also a part-time English teacher and a freelance educational consultant with a focus on diversity and inclusion.*

CHANGING THE MESSAGE

Tom Gagliano, North Brunswick, NJ

from *The Problem Was Me: How to End Negative Self-Talk and Take Your Life to a New Level*

Edited from the original.

As a child, if I dared to share my feelings or, God forbid cry, my father addressed me as his "little girl." This was a very damaging message that taught me to never share my feelings or my vulnerability with anyone. It affected my ability to develop intimacy with others when I became an adult. My father did eventually change his ways for the better, but we never had a close relationship.

When I arrived at the hospital near the end of his long battle with cancer, he looked very weak and frail. Although I felt sadness, I didn't know how to express my feelings to him because I had never felt safe with him. As I was ready to leave on one of his last days, he said to me, with a weak, tired voice, "Son, about twenty years ago my father was in the hospital dying of lung cancer. I was sitting right beside him, as you are seated beside me, and I could never find the courage to tell him I loved him or to share my feelings with him."

I became paralyzed with fear and sat back down, silent. In the midst of my father's physical pain, he was able to recognize my emotional pain. But, as he tried to reach out to me, my fear of intimacy awakened, warning me not to let my guard down.

My father was riddled with cancer, frail and weak, yet to me, he still had the power of a ten-foot giant. My mind said, "Run out of this room as fast as you can. Don't be vulnerable in front of him!" So I said nothing. I grasped my father's hand to say goodbye. He pulled me closer and began to weep.

The only time I had ever seen my father cry was when he was drunk and seeking forgiveness for being abusive. On the outside, I remained stoic as he wept. Inside, a horrible lump lodged in my throat. I could not tell my father I loved him.

I prayed to God for help. I'm a recovering addict and when there is this much pain, an addict will go one of two ways: to their addiction or to their support group. I didn't know which way I was going after I left my father's room. As I approached the hospital elevator, I saw a friend from one of the meetings I attended step out of the elevator. He happened to be visiting someone else in the hospital that night. Without thinking, I gave him a big hug. I needed to hold someone I could trust and this guy miraculously appeared. In time, as I grew spiritually, I recognized divine intervention had taken place that day in my life. God had shown up. My friend was sent to comfort me when I didn't know how to comfort myself. Without him, I might have chosen my addiction to ease my pain. I also would never have built up the courage to tell my father a few days later that I loved him.

Several years later, we had to put our dog to sleep. Our oldest son was the same age as the dog, and he was very attached to her. As we returned from the veterinarian's office, I noticed our son was sad and withdrawn.

"Is everything okay?" I asked him.

"I'm fine dad."

He did not look fine, so I asked him again, "Are you alright?"

"I'll be alright," He replied.

Instead of walking away and avoiding the emotions both of us were feeling, like my father did when I was a kid, I hugged him. His tears started to flow as his grip on me tightened. At that moment, I knew I was providing my son a safe place to cry in his father's arms, a place I didn't have as a kid. I was able to show him that it is acceptable to cry in the arms of his father. I never had a safe place to go as a child, but my children do because I have created a safe place for them to share their feelings, whatever those feelings are.

***Tom Gagliano** has worn many hats throughout his career. He started out as a successful entrepreneur but, at age 51 switched to pursue his dream of helping others. His book with Dr. Abraham Twerski,* The Problem Was Me: How to End Negative Self-Talk and Take Your Life to a New Level, *serves as a blueprint to help parents give their children the positive and healthy messages that may have been denied to them in their own childhood. Today Tom is a life coach, published author, and a keynote speaker with a Master's degree in social work. He is a regular on many radio networks and on the TBN television network.*

SEARCHING FOR DAD

Michael Cruse, Alexandria, VA

As much as I try to deny it, our son clearly has a preferred parent … daddy. In a perfect toddler world, his preference would be to have both parents within arm's reach at all times, but that's not always possible. If my wife needs to leave the house, our son will typically fuss a bit, he might even shed a tear or two. However, when I leave, like every morning for work, he starts screaming, heaving his body onto the floor, his arms and legs flailing about wildly.

It doesn't stop there. My son follows me from room to room when we're home, saying, "Ko Daddy" (aka "Come on Daddy") and "What'd you doing Daddy?" I think my wife actually gave birth to my second shadow. If I somehow manage to leave a room without him, he gets very whiny, nervous and scared, only to be relieved and all smiles when he sees me.

Sometimes his whining frustrates me, and at times I wonder out loud to my wife, "Why is he so upset? I'm right here." My wife always tells me how much he loves me (which I know), and how I'm his hero. She also tells me to put myself in his shoes; he feels lost without Daddy.

When she told me that, I reflected back on my relationship with my father, or more appropriately, the lack thereof, and one very pivotal time in my childhood where I felt very alone.

Over the years, people have inquired about my dad, as I have spent the majority of my time talking and writing about my mother and our abusive relationship. I never talked or wrote about my dad before, because the emotions were far more painful. They were born from a lack of his desire to know me, or even see me.

After a nasty divorce when I was just a toddler, my dad, who was in the Navy, went off and lived the Navy life as a single guy. This meant I rarely saw or heard from him. Many birthdays and holidays passed with little or no contact. He eventually remarried and had more children. I met him, and spent a small amount of time with him in my pre-teen years but, for the most part, our relationship was non-existent at best.

In early June of 1992, the week of my 8th grade graduation, my father was in San Diego (where I lived with my mother at the time) for some sort of naval training exercise. He called to let me know he was in town, but only for a few days.

I decided to go for broke and invited him to my graduation that week, stressing how I really would like him to come. He hesitated, but eventually agreed and mustered up a half-hearted response of excitement and sense of gratefulness for my invitation. I knew he was lying. I was a boy who had always silently yearned for male connection so I got my hopes up anyway.

My mom tried to be supportive; her attempts however, could not hide her massive skepticism. I didn't care; I knew he was coming.

The big day came. I still remember it like yesterday. My dad hadn't shown up by the time the pre-ceremony chit-chat and socializing were over. So what? I told myself. The important thing was that he would see me walk up and get my graduation certificate.

We all took our seats as the graduation ceremony began. Nervously shifting in my seat, I turned from side to side, looking back and forth, hoping to catch a glimpse of him as he arrived. Scanning every face in the crowd, eyes squinted by the bright California sun, I saw parents' faces full of pride and affection, but none of them belonged to me. Occasionally, I would catch a glimpse of my mom; a smile plastered on her face as if she had just swallowed bitter cough medicine. She was trying to convey pride and joy, but just under the mask of faux-happiness was a tornado of sadness, worry, and angst, along with a dash of "I told you so," as she watched me desperately search the crowd. I didn't care; I knew my dad was coming. I would not acknowledge her worry; I would not give her the satisfaction. This time she would be wrong.

The ceremony came and went like a flash. I stood and walked and returned to my seat. It went by so fast but I knew he was out there and he saw me even if I didn't see him.

As soon as all the pomp and circumstance concluded, we were released back to our parents. My mom found me so quickly: it was almost as if she materialized out of thin air. She was beaming with pride, tears in her eyes telling me how proud she was of me, and how much I had grown up, hugging me tightly; too tightly. That's when I knew. My father never arrived. Even though I knew the truth, the lonely, sad, boy inside would not be shoved aside this time. I blurted out, "Where's Dad? Did he see me?" My mother stared at me blankly for a moment, and just as I looked away, I spotted the slightest of smiles form on her face. Not only was she not sad, she was happy this had happened. Victory was hers.

So yes, my son hovers around and follows me from room to room. And yes, my son has to be involved in everything I'm doing. He bursts into the room on my mornings to sleep in and wakes me up by jumping on the bed, smothering me with hugs. My son whines when he can't see me, cries like a crazy person when I leave for work and gives me a super happy running hug with the scream of "DADDY!" when I get home.

I don't begrudge him for getting upset anymore; well I try not to at least. When he calls out, "Daddy, where are you?" I make sure to hug him a little tighter these days and tell him, "I'm here buddy"...because I always will be.

Michael Cruse *is a married father of one crazy, funny, over-the-top, beautiful toddler son. He is a life-long story-teller with a love for writing and the creator and lead writer at PapaDoesPreach.com currently still stuck in a nine-to-five job, but inching closer to his dream of being a writer when he grows up, one blog post at a time. Born and raised in San Diego, CA, he now resides in Alexandria, VA.*

SELLING FATHERHOOD

Chris Bernholdt, Devon, PA

My dad prided himself on the new sound system in our living room. It was packed with power. It had a turntable, a tape deck, and the newest feature, a compact disc player. When people would come over, he would ask them if they had ever heard *Bocelli* in surround sound. He would then crank the music higher than necessary and watch their reaction, rapt, looking for that moment when the person's mind was blown. Although, really, it might have been their eardrums bursting from the carefully maintained equalizer.

Each Christmas, we would spend it with the extended family. His three brothers and their families would often congregate at our house or at my aunt's house with an overflowing mound of presents, so deep we could barely see the Christmas tree. All of us we would get dressed up and attend *The Nutcracker*. When we returned to our house the year after my father bought that sound system, we were "treated" to *The Nutcracker Suite* at a sound decibel, as usual, much higher than necessary. He then left the room and headed to his bedroom.

What happened next changed my perception of my dad forever. He emerged, wearing only his long underwear and began prancing around like a ballerina, pirouetting like only an ungraceful man can do. I never laughed so hard in my life. He quickly bowed and exited stage left down the hallway while we cheered "Encore! Encore!"

He is still like that with almost everything. Growing up in his house meant he would draw attention to experiences and people, never the things you had or wanted. Meals made by him would become "the best tacos I ever had" and he would sell them to you like you were a customer at his food truck instead of sitting at his kitchen table.

Family vacations were about adventures. Like the time he took us to California and just had to show us the La Brea tar pits which, for some reason, were closed. He insisted, despite the warning sign, we take a picture to prove we were there and pose like we were actually disappointed.

My dad never wore shorts. For the longest time I wasn't sure if he even owned a pair. At Disney World he was in slacks and a business casual, button down shirt with no tie. He would be making calls on the payphone between rides and would fit those calls in when he could, furiously scribbling notes into a tiny book he kept on his clients, the early version of a pocket-sized smart phone.

My dad was and still is a salesman in every way. For example, he will try to get you to eat the last hot dog. You can protest you don't have room for it yet, somehow, you will eat it. As a kid, I remember how he shook hands with everyone he met looking them in the eye when he did. He never forgot anyone's name and would call people out from behind desks to show off my brothers or me.

He was not the dad sitting by the pool with the paper, barely paying attention to his kids. He was the dad on top of the inflatable alligator my younger brother and I insisted we had to have on vacation for the hotel pool. He was the guy who led a rousing rendition of *On Top of Old Smokey* in front of numerous other people at Lost Land Lake. He was the dad on the floor, in the trenches, always playing with his kids.

He showed me how to be a dad without website and parenting blogs telling him how. I suppose that's why I want to emulate him with my own children, remembering how he would lay on the floor and help me put my GI Joe toys together while listening to an AM radio that was never an arm's length away. The way he cared for us, the way he played with us, and the way he loved us was the perfect example of what it meant to be a dad.

He is still the same dad to this day with my own children. They know Grandpa B will do anything for a laugh. He dresses up in goofy costumes, plays inside pop up tents, and will get down on the floor with them.

Now, in the play kitchen, he's trying to sell those fake chicken nuggets to my youngest daughter. But it is me who is buying today, and every day, from him as his best customer.

A long time ago, he sold me on fatherhood, hook, line, and sinker.

Chris Bernholdt *is the creator of www.DadNCharge.com where he writes about creativity with kids and empowers dads to embrace their role in modern fatherhood. His writing has appeared on The Huffington Post, The Good Men Project, and Life of Dad. He is a stay-at-home dad to three kids ages nine, seven, and four and lives in the Philadelphia area with his wife Susie. Chris is the co-founder of Philly Dads Group and a board member of the National At Home Dad Network. Two of his stories also appeared in* Dads Behaving DADLY: 67 Truths, Tears and Triumphs of Modern Fatherhood.

PART TWO

BECOMING DAD

"When you first pick up your newborn child, the miracle of it is overwhelming."
- Jock McMillan, father of five sons from Shropshire, UK

IT'S HIM

Henry Amador-Batten, Durham, NC

I can still, so vividly, remember the day I received the photo. It came via text message. I emailed it to myself in order to get a larger look.

I opened the image and looked at it with a mixture of amazement, fear and disbelief.

A few moments later I shared it with my husband.

"Look what she sent me," I said, "a sonogram photo."

"It's him."

We both spent a few silent moments gazing at the image.

We had not even met the woman on the other end of the text. I had only exchanged a few polite messages with her up to that point.

An acquaintance of ours was related to this young woman. She knew we had been trying to grow our family and she knew her sister had not wanted to grow hers.

Rather than play the middleman, she asked her sister if she could give us her number, to which, she agreed.

I sat with that number for nearly a full day.

You would have thought I would have jumped on it, but I didn't, I sat. What would I say to her? I heard you wanted to give up your baby?

What a tiny approach to such a giant thought.

Do I bring up the fact that we were two married men now?

What if that crushes our hopes? What if that idea is unacceptable to her?

I was so consumed by all the questions that I just sat there, frozen and fearful, two adjectives I would have never used to describe myself before that day. But this situation, this opportunity, had the potential of shaking all the leaves from my tree.

If it worked out, my life - our lives - would never be the same. And it was that truth that turned me into a scared, still man.

I eventually mustered up the nerve to text her. I introduced myself, took a shot at a sincere attempt at understanding her incredibly difficult decision and thanked her for considering us. She responded quickly, and after a few exchanges, asked when we would like to get together.

Thank God the ice was broken.

I suddenly felt safe behind my phone and asked if it could be soon. It had dawned on me that if this was going to happen, we would have to be proactive and quick. I already knew she had tried to abort this child but she was too far along. I also knew she had reached out to an adoption agency.

If we were going to have a chance at convincing her we would be the perfect family for her unborn baby, we would have very little time to waste. We agreed to meet at a coffee house the next afternoon.

"Would you like to see a picture of recent sonogram?" she texted next.

I said yes.

And there we were, my husband and I, looking at this little forming stranger who suddenly entered our lives like a cold rush of air though a crack in a window.

In the privacy of our home, without having yet met the woman carrying him, we were looking at his photo.

I asked my husband how he felt. He seemed thoughtful and quiet and said he wasn't sure.

What if this is the first time we're looking at our son? We both wondered.

What if this is the first of our one million photos of him?

Shouldn't we be excited?

Happy?

Should we tell anybody?

Should we forward this picture to your mother?

What if she's going to be a grandmother?

Truthfully, we weren't happy. We were too afraid to embrace the happiness.

We didn't share the news. As a matter of fact, there were many people in our circle who knew nothing until the day we brought that five-pound baby boy home from the hospital.

There were so many variables, so many what-ifs between the moment of possibility and the lofty, far away idea of him actually being ours.

What if we can't afford the adoption?

What if she doesn't like us?

What if she changes her mind?

What if, God forbid, something happens to the baby?

What if … what if … what if …?

We were so lost in the uncertainties that we lost sight of the dream, our dream.

On that amazing day, we were indeed looking into our baby's face for the very first time.

He soon would be ours! He is ours!

And out of all the millions of pictures we will take of our beautiful boy, this first photo, our first photo, will always mean more than you could possibly understand.

Henry Amador-Batten *lives in Durham, North Carolina and is a strong advocate for the LGBTQ community. He lives with his husband and their three-year-old son. He and his husband were the first same-sex couple to jointly adopt a child in Broward County Florida — setting legal precedence. He is a certified Holistic Life Coach and specializes in teaching advanced life skills. Henry is also the founding mind behind parenting blog, DADsquared, and has developed it into an amazing resource and support destination for gay dads and dads to be. Learn more at www.dadsquared.org.*

LOSING MURRAY

Matt Duvall, Annville, PA

Losing a baby.

I want to make a joke about it, like, it's just like losing your car keys or maybe something about being absent-minded … but that's a defense mechanism. It's how I deal with the arbitrary, soul-crushing stuff that just happens when there's no villain and nobody to blame.

As I'm composing my first draft of this, I'm lying in bed. My son woke up early this morning because of a cold, so he's now nestled in between my wife and me, sleeping soundly, his arm thrown over his eyes and his head pressed into me. He's two and a half, funny, smart, and kindhearted. Our daughter, six-weeks-old, is lying in her bassinet, making some sort of grunting noise, as infants do. She has started smiling regularly at me when I talk to her, which shows she already has an advanced sense of humor. This is my family, my rock, and even when I'm not sure of anything else in my life, I am sure of them and of our love for each other. We call ourselves "Team Duvall," half-jokingly, but that's really how it feels.

Four years ago, at almost exactly the time I am writing this, my wife and I were imagining what our soon-to-be-expanded family would be like. Did we hope for a boy or a girl? We went back and forth on that one. Would s/he be hairy like me? Which features would s/he get from each of us? We did the intake forms at the OBGYN practice, had the sample formula tins lined up like little soldiers on the counter. We only told our parents because it was still early, but we were excited, happy and a little nervous. We had songs already for the baby – "I throw my hand buds in the air sometimes, saying Ay-yo."

The day of THE check-up, I had to go back to the school where I taught to do some tutoring. Right before I had to leave, they were putting the little portable heart rate monitor on my wife's stomach. I hoped to hear our baby's heart beat for the first time, but there was nothing but static.

"It's ok," the nurse assured us. "They're so small now, sometimes we can't find it."

I wasn't worried. I left and went to tutoring. The students weren't happy to be there, but I sure was. I was going to be a dad! I had put my phone on silent, because why wouldn't I? I wouldn't need to be poised for news for another seven or eight months. Then I'd need it on at work so I could rush to the hospital to see the little guy or gal come into the world.

That's why I missed the call from my mother-in-law. I listened to the voicemail as I left school. I was numb. I didn't know what to feel.

There was blood work to be done, just to confirm what the emergency ultrasound had already shown.

Each pregnancy has a one in 1,000 chance of being a molar pregnancy, one in which an empty egg somehow gets fertilized. It's not viable, and can become cancerous, spreading throughout the mother's body. In extreme cases it can lead to death.

Our baby wasn't going to ever be a she or a he. We would never hold it, never comfort it through its first fever, never kiss a boo boo, never teach it to ride a bike.

Instead, my wife had to have surgery, and then follow up care for months to make sure there was no malignant tissue anywhere.

We were devastated. Everything seemed dull and grey to me. My wife and I supported each other through the grief, pain, anger – the whole spectrum of emotions - but we dealt with them in completely different ways. My wife wanted to tell those around us, to explain what had happened. I couldn't deal with the platitudes or assurances of some greater plan, so I didn't tell anyone. I tried to work more, so I wouldn't think about it, but I'm sure that year I was not a very effective teacher. I was angry a lot. I exercised more. I avoided talking about it, except to my wife, but I couldn't avoid thinking about it. When that stupid "Ay-yo" song would come on the radio, I changed stations.

In retrospect, my wife was right. I should have told people. The platitudes are annoying, but they're what we have in order to let people know we care. And sometimes, just sharing that pain can help us recover.

Four years have passed. I don't know if I can ever be over it. I'm not angry about it anymore, though. I am still sad for the possibilities we never got to realize, but I have so much good to be grateful for that I can't be negative about the past.

So, here is where my big takeaway should go. I wrote this because I wanted to share how an event like this affects fathers too, because when we lost Murray the Molar (our gallows humor attempt to make things better), I looked for information and online groups for fathers and found one abandoned WordPress site. I want people to know that dads suffer too when our partners lose a baby. It's a different kind of suffering, but no less legitimate. We may deal with it in different ways, but it is still real. Hemingway said "the world breaks everyone and afterward many are strong at the broken places. But those that will not break it kills."

Sometimes it's okay — better, even — to be broken.

Matt Duvall *is the father of a two-and-a-half-year-old boy and a 4-month-old girl. He is also a former professional wrestler who appeared on national TV shows as his alter ego, The Prince of Polyester. He completed his MFA at Seton Hill University, which is also where he met his wife, Natalie. He is currently a PhD student at Drexel University's School of Education and primary caregiver for his children. When he's not reading about theories of learning or changing diapers, he practices Krav Maga and Brazilian jiu jitsu, runs, and tries to avoid mowing the yard. He blogs (infrequently) at really-crankydad.wordpress.com.*

FATUM INTERVENERIT

(FATE INTERVENED)

Jason Greene, Astoria, NY

My wife and I confidently drove over the George Washington Bridge in a truck full of belongings and big dreams. We didn't know anyone in New York City, but that didn't worry us. My wife was beginning law school and I was going to be the next great Broadway star. Jobs were hard to come by, so I worked in Human Resources and retail jobs while auditioning in any spare moments I could find. I believed it was only a matter of time before someone would discover my talents as an actor, skyrocketing me to the next awards show stage.

My confidence, or I should say "cockiness," increased after taking an acting class where I was praised by established directors, writers, and actors. On one occasion, a highly successful director told me, "your so F-ing good! You'll make it someday." I wasn't the only one in the class, of course. There were about ten of us, but one classmate (I'll call him "Breorge Cloonpitt") and I always landed the juiciest roles. I played characters experiencing a wide range of emotions and "Breorge" played the straight man. We were always in competition with each other as to who would be the star of the class.

Then, f*atum intervenerit* (fate intervened).

Once a season I had to work an overnight shift at a retail store and switch all of the displays around. It was a tiring job and I would drag my weary body into bed the morning after. And, since I hated that job, I was always in a bad mood after those long nights. On this particular day, I wanted to fall asleep quickly because my wife and I had tickets to see David Letterman and I wanted to be rested for the show. My wife came into our bedroom and sat beside me. I immediately became annoyed. She poked my back. I told her to leave me alone because I was tired. I needed to sleep and whatever she felt was so important would have to wait. Then she patted me again. I begrudgingly sat up in bed with a disgusted look on my face and asked, "What is so important?"

She answered with two words that changed my life forever: "I'm pregnant."

As the day went along, I did everything in a daze. I stared aimlessly off in the distance and coasted along. When my wife and I arrived at the Ed Sullivan Theater to pick up our tickets, we sort of stuck out our hands to receive them. When they asked if we were excited to be there, we both mumbled dazed responses. I don't remember much about the show, but actor Alec Baldwin and soccer phenom Freddie Adu were the guests and Cindy Lauper sang. Also, I remember David Letterman swore before the show and everyone laughed. That is all I remember from the show; my mind was elsewhere.

When my son was born, I had to make a choice as to where my life was going. The acting life consists of auditioning at all times of the day, long shoots that seem never-ending and, my least favorite thing of all, networking. Actors attend parties where they meet people and talk about how great they are. That became hard to do – not because I didn't think I was great, but because, unlike my colleagues, I had a poop-filled diaper with my name on it waiting for me at home. The nightlife had to go, and soon, everything else that went with it. We made the decision that it would be best if I stayed at home with the kids while my wife started her legal career. I've watched her career blossom, as well as my former classmates'. They've gone on to join Saturday Night Live and appear on Broadway, TV, and in films. I would be lying if there wasn't a hint of jealousy inside me as I have watched them all prosper. I'm aware my kids love having their daddy around and I love every minute spent with them. But there are those moments when I can't help but wonder, "what if?"

My story isn't that different from that of most stay-at-home parents. For one reason or another, we made the choice to stay home. That choice comes with trade-offs; we get to watch our children grow up right before our eyes, but we also have to watch others pass us by. How do we get through those moments of depression and jealousy? For me, I only have to look at the faces of my three kids to know I am making the right choice for them.

Currently, I am acting again in New York City. It's a small, intimate setting and seating is limited. Those in attendance get to see my wide range of emotions and hear my wide range of dialects as I bring various literary characters to life. It doesn't pay, but the audience assures me I'm twenty times better than every other person in my old acting class. If you're lucky, and you happen to know someone who knows someone, you may be able to score a ticket. Just bring a pillow, because the floor in my kids' room starts to feel pretty hard after a while. And if you happen to say to me, "you're so F-ing good!" I'll have to wash your mouth out with soap.

Jason Greene *is a former actor and playwright living in New York City who now focuses his time on being a stay-at-home dad. He writes about life and raising his three kids at www.OneGoodDad.com. One of his stories also appeared in* Dads Behaving DADLY: 67 Truths, Tears and Triumphs of Modern Fatherhood.

CRY OF VICTORY

Adam Rust, Covington, KY

Life has a way of thwarting the best-laid plans.

Sometimes, we have better experiences or learn better lessons from the detours of life's journey than we would have had from a clearly planned route. This truth came into sharper focus for me during the recent birth of our fifth child. My wife and I had planned a home birth, assisted by a midwife. Not everything went according to plan.

We had birthed all four of our previous children at home with midwives. I had the incredible privilege of catching all four of those precious children as they made their transition from a dark and watery world to the world of air and light. Having this previous experience made me fairly proficient in assisting my wife as she performed the miracle of birth. She handles it like a boss. She is a miracle worker!

I went into this fifth birth confident we could handle the twists and turns of the birthing process. Nevertheless, we still wanted the support of a midwife along the way. There is much benefit in having a good midwife who has a thorough knowledge of the particular woman and baby, capable of handling all the prenatal care and assisting with the birth.

Things escalated quickly once my wife went into labor. Only a few minutes after calling the midwife, I was back on the phone with her again, telling her I could see the crown. She offered to stay on the phone with me to coach me through what would happen next because the baby was coming faster than her. I paused to consider my options. We could keep the phone on speaker and listen to the distracting road noise through the midwife's phone as she drove, or I could hang up and give my wife my complete and undivided attention and support. I declined the midwife's offer and hung up the phone.

We were on our own.

Well, not totally alone. We had our two eldest daughters (ages seven and five) in the room with us and a friend was also present to help out and take photos. Even so, we would be doing this without a trained professional in the room. I had another decision to make. I could panic and give into the fear I might do something wrong or I could stay calm, square my shoulders, stiffen my spine and be the rock my wife needed in that moment. I chose the latter.

Over the next thirty minutes, I listened to every breath she took and every sound she made. I watched her every movement and read every signal. I said only a few words to help keep her breathing rhythm and to encourage her in the amazing job she was doing.

She bore down for a big push. The head was out. She pushed again and I felt a warm, slippery weight in my hands. It seemed for a few seconds like every sound died out and everything else in the room vanished. Even my own breathing stopped. I was only aware of my wife and our new little baby. I was awe-struck. His strong, shrill cry snapped me back to reality and I heard my wife's voice as she started talking to him. She and I worked together to maneuver the baby into a position where he could nurse. Our daughters were sitting at the foot of the bed with looks of utter delight beaming from their faces. "Our new brother is here!" they exclaimed.

The midwife arrived about ten minutes after the baby was born. I was glad to see her because I didn't know much about the afterbirth procedure. While she attended to the baby, my wife and I basked in the afterglow of the miracle that had happened.

As we admired his miniature digits massaging the blanket and listened to his little gasps in between mouthfuls of milk, our daughters asked us questions.

"Mommy, did that hurt?"

"It hurt for a little while, but I'm fine now."

"Dad were you scared?"

I paused to think. "Well, I thought about being scared," I said. "But then I thought about what mom needed and I realized I couldn't be scared because it wouldn't help her at all. We had to work together as a team to get the job done. I couldn't help mom and be scared at the same time, so I just focused on her and the baby. What about you? Were you scared?"

"Not really. It was kind of sad to watch her be in pain," they replied.

We all hugged each other. It was the pinnacle moment of solidarity and teamwork in our family.

Teamwork is something we talk about frequently in our family. I want teamwork to be a value that shapes our household. This birth has become the example we recall when we are talking about what teamwork looks like when we are working on chores around the house, going on hikes, traveling together, and even going to bed.

The shared experience of this birth also showed our daughters their mother's unparalleled strength, which gives them confidence as they look ahead to being mothers themselves some day. They learned that their father will always be present and invested in his family. If dad didn't get scared and run away when the contractions got closer together and bodily fluids started gushing everywhere, then he surely won't take off at the first sign of any other challenge.

Had everything about this birth gone according to plan, I would not have been able to demonstrate this truth to my family so vividly. But thanks to the departure from the plan, my family knows now, more than ever, I will be there for everything with them.

Adam Rust *is husband to his wonderful wife and father to his five amazing, fun, and thoroughly interesting children. Adam once thought he never wanted to be a father. Now he finds his greatest joy in life in the everyday moments of fatherhood. By day, he works at a video production company called Epipheo. By night, he shares his reflections on fatherhood at www.fathervision.com. He is also chief content curator at www.dailyedify.com.*

FIRST FEEDING

Christopher Bakker, Chicago, IL

My son could not eat. I took the news like a hammer to my chest.

My wife's letdown reflex after the delivery did not happen on time. My son's greenish meconium came and went but she still could not produce breast milk. Our doula was giving a post-natal massage to my wife Nancy to encourage the first colostrum. Nothing. He sucked at her breast to stimulate oxytocin. Nothing. Nurses were frowning and threatening formula and Nancy was close to tears. I stood there, useless.

My son could not eat!

And there was nothing I could do about it.

The birth had not gone well. The birth canal was too small. We had to have an emergency C-section, putting us both on edge. The hospital had my wife on an operating table and seven pounds of slick, pinkish seal-like goo was lifted out of my wife before I could get the scrubs on to the nurse's satisfaction. I missed nearly all of it, and I was upset. His Apgar score was fine. In the post-natal warming table, his little face scrunched at me like a wizened old man. His calf muscles looked like a pro soccer player's from kicking in the womb for months on end.

I have a son.

I have a son!

And he could not eat.

His first meal would be formula. I felt like I was letting my wife down somehow. I was starting to sink into a quicksand of self-doubt about my parenting abilities because I could not fix this, my first parenting challenge. The doctors and nurses seemed to lose their bedside manner and were threatening to take our child and feed him. They were going to do what I so clearly could not. Tears rolled down Nancy's face as they left the room each time with their threats of quicker action than us new parents.

Then, our wonderful doula, Tara, and one of the nurses came up with an idea: I was going to breastfeed him.

Uh... what?!

They explained that they had a gravity drip device. They could strap a small, thin tube to my tiniest finger. It would allow the child to nurse from a finger and bond with a parent when the letdown response had not come yet. For whatever reason, the oxytocin was not allowing her mammary tissue to produce milk.

Fine. Strap it to me!

My pinkie finger was rigged up and they handed him to me.

I had never held an infant, let alone fed one. I began to shiver like a cold wind had blown through me. What if I did this wrong?

I felt like horses were trampling my guts, stifling my will to breathe.

I took a deep breath. I could do this.

They laid my son gently in my arms. His smell was intoxicating. I gave him my pinkie finger wrapped up with the tiny tube. My baby boy, Pierce, nursed from my finger for the first meal of his life. He had formula. As he ate, he looked into my eyes. I swore he knew my face, recognizing my voice as the one that sang to him for months in the womb. Twelve hours later, Nancy's milk came in and she was able to breastfeed him.

Years later I would come to know the sweetness of his hugs, the joy of his resistance and the uniqueness of his ideas. I would understand the feelings other parents had told me but, until then, were unknown to me.

And, I discovered I could be a dad.

***Christopher Bakker** is a stay-at-home dad to a rambunctious seven-year-old. He writes grants for non-profits, schools, hospitals, and father groups. He is currently writing a book for Dads called The At-Home Dad Manual: How to Make Your Mark. He is proud to be a member of the National At-Home Dad Network and City Dads Group. When asked what he does, he is proud to list his biggest accomplishment, "I am a father."*

TWO BLUE LINES

Al Ferguson, Tunbridge Wells, Kent, UK

Miscarriage is a mysterious and devastating thing. I don't think dads talk about their experiences of miscarriage enough. The presumption is that a miscarriage happens to the mom, but I believe it happens to both parents. Both moms and dads feel a range of emotions when it happens, which, unfortunately, is quite common. And, unfortunately, it happened to us.

My wife and I had planned to get pregnant and could not have been happier when we saw the two blue lines.

It was during week six when the storm began. My wife found a small amount of blood. We quickly Googled in order to learn more about spotting, which we found is common during early pregnancy. As nervous first-time parents, we booked an appointment at the emergency scan department of the hospital just to be sure.

We sat in a corridor, opposite the ultrasound room, waiting our turn. Women and couples went into the room with anxious looks on their faces and came out either gleefully holding a baby scan picture or crying. We sat there, wondering our fate: overjoyed or distraught? We ended up feeling neither. It was too early to tell if we had a viable pregnancy. The ultrasound tech booked us for another scan in two weeks. The heartbeat would definitely be seen by then (or not), we were told.

When we returned two weeks later, we learned the fetus had grown but there was still no visible heartbeat. No one could explain it and no one could confirm viability. We lived the following weeks on edge, anxious, worried and hopeful. All the while this was happening, we were planning our wedding for the end of the summer. What should have been an exciting time of preparations for us was overcast by a darkening cloud of uncertainty and potential devastation.

A few days before our pre-wedding honeymoon was our third scan. Still no heartbeat but more growth! The doctor said, because of the growth, she couldn't definitively say we would lose the baby, but gave us a 95 percent chance of miscarriage at any point.

The Tuesday before the wedding, we endured another visit in the emergency scan waiting room. We hid ourselves from the other patients and braced for what would more than likely be bad news. This time, there was still no heartbeat but also no growth. We were told it was only a matter of time before her body rejected the unviable fetus and the miscarriage began. We had two options: let the miscarriage happen naturally, possibly during the wedding or opt for a D&C (Dilation and Curettage, a surgical procedure to remove the fetus) and thus cancel the wedding.

We decided to continue on with the wedding. If the miscarriage started, we'd cross that bridge when we came to it. The situation put everything into perspective. It helped us focus on us, and ironically, amongst the sadness, we had never been so close. We got married with tremendous intimacy between us.

Three days after the wedding, the miscarriage started. It began as a pain in my wife's abdomen. She knew it was happening. We called for our fifth emergency appointment. The bleeding was constant and she had continuous pain. I felt useless and inadequate, unable to do anything to comfort my wife's physical or emotional pain.

Seven weeks of uncertainty, hope and despair had come to an end. It was gut wrenching. As they wheeled my wife out of the room to do the D&C, I felt like my heart was being pulled out on the gurney too. I couldn't be with her when she was terrified. I wanted to comfort her, hold her hand and be there for her. Instead, I was in a cold room with just my thoughts for company.

Following the procedure, it was so hard to know how to act. I was devastated, but held it in. I wanted to be strong and look after my wife, who was heart-broken. I felt my tears would just add to her pain. This was a mistake. When I let my guard down and finally shared my feelings with her, it led to one of the best moments of our relationship. We both held each other and together, felt the pain. A new, unspoken connection grew between us. It is in these difficult, overcast situations when relationships can mature. For that, I am thankful.

Nearly two years have passed. I look back on that time with unexpected positivity. It could have ruined our relationship and any chance of building a healthy family together, but we turned it into a positive experience. My wife and I are stronger, more intimate and more open with each other. We made a conscious decision to keep trying and a year after our miscarriage, we welcomed our son into this world.

My hope is, through reading about my experience, it opens the door for other men to talk openly with their partners when they experience a miscarriage. The pain of a miscarriage happens to both parents. And it can be a mysterious and devastating thing.

Al Ferguson *is married to the beautiful Jen and father to a little boy. Al started www.thedadnetwork.co.uk to promote and encourage the role of dads within family life. The Dad Network follows his journey as a dad on this new adventure. Hopefully, it gives a fresh and humorous perspective into the world of being an expecting/new dad. Al lives in Kent in the UK.*

HOW TO RAISE A GIRL

Pat Jacobs, Elk Grove, IL

Any day now, I will be the father of a baby girl and I'll be honest, I'm terrified!

As a stay-at-home dad, it has become soberingly clear that the responsibility of raising this little girl is resting on my overweight shoulders. I'm a boy. I have a boy. I have been raising my boy to be like a boy. A girl is no boy.

Raising a boy is easy. My boy thinks atomic elbow drops are hysterical. When either of us makes a fart noise, we're the funniest two boys on the planet. Is it all going to change when this little girl comes into our daily routine? Can I give a girl an atomic elbow drop? Is it alright to teach her how to make farting sounds? Can I fart around a baby girl?!

These are legitimate parenting concerns for a boy who has been raising a boy and any day will be raising a girl. It will be like diving into a pool of freezing water. I want to be prepared. So one night, I ask my wife how I am supposed to raise our girl to be like a girl. She looked at me like the idiot I am and asks, "What the hell does 'like a girl' even mean?"

Marrying my wife is the smartest decisions I ever made.

My wife is the first person in my life who was able to break down the emotional walls I had up for over thirty years. She forced me to communicate by asking every hard question she could. She asked about my previous marriage, my childhood, how I was hurt, and how I hurt people. She helped me see how holding in my emotions would only keep me from seeing what was right in front of me.

I was reminded that night what an amazing woman I married. She is ambitious, willing to speak her mind, confident, and funny. She is passionate about her career, proud of where she is in life, and can spike a volleyball harder than anyone I've ever seen. She is a woman I am proud to spend the rest of my life with, even though she doesn't get my 1980's references and still hasn't seen The Godfather.

My wife is everything I want my little girl to be. She is everything I want both of my children to be. All I have to do is mix in a little of the man I have become, add a couple elbow drops and a sprinkle of some hysterical fart noises, and we will be just fine.

I've realized that raising a child to be intelligent, secure, confident, and emotionally stable has nothing to do with gender. I do not need to raise my daughter any differently than I have been raising her brother. I will not raise her with a softer touch, a more sensitive demeanor or a heightened sense of caution. I will raise her in the only way I know how - as my child.

Pat Jacobs *has been a stay-at-home dad for two years to his two-year-old son and nine-month-old daughter. He lives in the Chicago area with his amazingly talented and extremely supportive wife. Pat managed restaurants before deciding he would stay home. During nap time, he co-manages the www.JustaDad247.com blog to help stay-at-home dads find resources, humor, and support throughout their days. The Beatles are the soundtrack of his life. Two of his stories also appeared in* Dads Behaving DADLY: 67 Truths, Tears and Triumphs of Modern Fatherhood.

MOURNING MY CHILDREN

Lucas Grindley, Los Angeles, CA

For me, the first step to becoming a dad was letting my kids return from the dead. I had killed the idea of them years ago. I was the Grinch who stole the picket fence and the puppy and packed it up in some heavy mental baggage.

To illustrate how far my perspective has swung in the opposite direction, I have to admit I often have an irrational panic that someone will come take them away. I'm so attached now to my twin girls that it doesn't feel insincere, for example, to cheer after one of them pees in the potty. I don't even feel weird about how often I'm trapped in everyday conversations involving their bowels movements and what it looked like, and whether there's a rash, and what the rash looks like. All of these previously unconscionable details are now the quite minor cost of doing business, as it were, if you want a family.

But, like I imagine it is for a lot of gay men, once upon a time, I had forcibly stopped myself from thinking I would have a son or daughter. I erased their "memory" before they ever existed.

One particularly depressing day while I sat in my car, parked a short walk from my college dorm room, I tried reconciling coming out with the traditional picture I had expected for my life. I realized I'd have to scratch out those kids from the picture. In writing classes, they call this "killing your darlings" — which is shorthand for editing out any plot line that stunts the story's development. In life, I think they call it "crushing your dreams."

In defense of my ice-villain inclinations, though, being fully myself had become more important than having kids — or having any family at all, really. Already I had trained myself to live with the risk my parents or friends might push me away when I came out (even though they didn't). I mourned a million possible tragedies, few of which came to fruition. One I certainly mourned was my children.

It used to be when you came out people would stop asking you about getting married or having kids. Everyone immediately "gets it," that you can't.

Nathan never got it, though.

I'm not sure if it came up on the first date, but I can't remember a time when I was not aware Nathan wanted to have kids. He is a K-12 music teacher, which is simultaneously encouraging and intimidating. I feel better knowing he's sort of a natural with kids. Next to him, I look like a hack.

Nathan is in sync with kids. When the girls tell daddy to *please, pretty please* play the *Frozen* song for the car ride, I've caught Papa concealing a smile because he wants to hear it again too. He has taught rooms filled with little kindergarteners, getting them all to sing along and perform adorable choral-ography. I've got enough trouble getting our two toddlers to follow me down a hallway.

Before the girls arrived, my parenting experience was intentionally limited. Part of me felt it wasn't a muscle worth exercising since I would never have kids. I concede to having been a bit aloof around my friends' children. I'd smile and wave in a way that hid my real concern about what would happen next if that kid actually came over and wanted to play. I'm not sure anyone who knew me then would have felt comfortable letting me babysit without Nathan present. Maybe that was my insecurity talking. I'm told all parents think they will quite possibly be terrible parents.

While it was still "just us," I always told Nathan we would have kids — one day. To be honest, I didn't believe it could ever happen, but I knew it wasn't possible to stay with him otherwise.

And, it's not like I was opposed to the whole idea, not really. I just needed time to let it sink in, this expectation that I might prefer tossing aside a life filled with quiet dinners and nights at the theater, or trips to Vegas or jaunts to Rehoboth Beach. Don't let anyone tell you otherwise: your life will change when you decide to have kids. If you think seeing a movie is expensive now, try throwing in a babysitter who charges by the hour. Disney is our new Vegas. I shop more often at Baby Gap than Banana Republic.

I told myself stalling on having children was fine because I wasn't ready to have kids at 25 or 27 or even 30. I had things to do! But the more I think about it, the more I realize I was dragging my feet so I'd have time to re-imagine my life — yet again.

Now every day starts with the noise of the baby monitor. "Daddy, Daddy," it sometimes begins like a gentle song. Then it crescendos. "DADDY!" And then if I roll over, "DAAAADYYYY!" There is really no sleeping in. I can bring the girls back to our bed and wishfully think they'll just quietly snuggle. But, if it's past 7 a.m., the girls have things to tell you about and books to read and breakfast to eat, juice to drink, Dora to explore with, and more books and more food and more juice and more Dora.

Yes, life can get monotonous. We call it a "schedule." Everything happens every day at the same time in the same order — at least if things are going well.

Maybe parenting doesn't sound appealing. It would not have sounded appealing to me years ago. But I wouldn't have been able to imagine life as a parent then. I'm unexpectedly proud of my girls for little things, like learning to jump, and I sort of melt when they hug each other, and you can't imagine the magnitude of melting when they hug me instead. They really do blow kisses when I leave for work, and they really do scream my name deliriously when coming in the door from work, rushing forward to show me a picture they drew with crayons.

I had forgotten all of that would happen. And I no longer pretend I didn't want it.

***Lucas Grindley** is Editorial Director for Here Media and VP, Editorial Director of* The Advocate, *the leading source of up-to-date and extensive LGBT News. He lives in Los Angeles with his husband and daughters. Follow him on Twitter @lucasgrindley and on Instagram @lucasgrindley.*

DRAWING THE LINE

Kevin Zelenka, Henderson, NV

As I sat between two incubators in the Level 3 NICU and looked at my newborn sons, tubes in their tiny arms and oxygen being pumped into their little noses, I wanted nothing more in the world than to bring two healthy boys home. I wondered if I would.

When they decided to show up five weeks early, I was scared. Not scared of raising the "double trouble team" as I call them now, but scared maybe one of them would not make it home. I'm not, and have never been, very religious, but there were a couple times during their stay in the NICU that I made a pit stop at the chapel on my way back to my wife's room. Once, I broke down and sobbed. I cried my eyes out. I even prayed. All I asked was that if I couldn't bring home two healthy sons, then I needed some help dealing with and accepting it.

I had already quit my job in preparation for my upcoming role as a stay-at-home dad, so I was able to be in the hospital as long as it took to get everyone home. Every three hours my wife pumped breast milk and I would deliver it to the NICU nurses, sometimes in stocking feet. The twins were more than little. They were tiny. Not as small as some (5lb-4oz and 3lbs-13oz), but still a lot smaller than I thought they would be when I dreamed of my wife and I holding them for the first time. The only images my imagination had to go by were the babies I saw on television, who were eight pounds with a full head of hair and never cried. Combined, our sons were that size.

After two weeks of observation, one twin came home. Six weeks later, our second was released and our family was complete.

It has been a wild ride ever since. The smaller twin, the one I shed so many tears over, is now walking around the house when he's not running. He has non-stop energy and does not like to go to sleep. His brother, who wasn't much bigger upon birth, is the climber of the family and will soon be auditioning for a Tarzan re-make.

It's exciting and overwhelming to see how far they have come. My little fragile offspring have become full-fledged toddlers and sometimes it's hard to watch. Knowing when to step in and "save" them and when to just let them learn from their bumps and bruises is difficult, especially considering their once fragile state.

Growing up, my brother and I were prohibited from playing around the machinery that operated on our farm, so we played in the sandbox next to the garage for hours and hours, coming in the house a couple shades darker than when we had left from a mixture of sun and dirt. We'd make bows and arrows with branches and yarn, sharpening sticks by rubbing them on the cement stoop to use as makeshift arrows. We rode our bikes as fast as we could on the gravel road in front of our property. I can't even count the number of times I got the wind knocked out of me by falling out of one of the trees bordering our yard.

Looking back, it seemed like maybe my parents put in place a set of boundaries without us even realizing it. We weren't afforded the opportunity to cripple ourselves, and yet we still had the ability to be kids and explore. Our imaginations grew as we developed miniature cities in the sand with our Matchbox cars and Tonka trucks. We battled pirates and other assorted "bad guys" with our bows and arrows, chasing them on the two wheels of our make-believe horses.

I want to give my sons these same opportunities to explore and adventure, even if it means emptying a few Band-Aid boxes. Considering where they started, however, I find myself wanting to wrap them in bubble wrap. My parents knew how to draw the line between keeping my brother and I safe and smothering our creativity. I don't. I know I need to give my sons more freedom, like I had, but I find it difficult to do so. I flashback to the tubes and wires keeping my twins alive any time they do anything. As far as my boys have come, I still have a long way to go.

Kevin Zelenka *and his wife hit the jackpot with twin toddlers two years ago. He and his wife enjoy living in sunny Las Vegas where they raise their sons and their dog, making it a full house. When he's not leading his boys on another adventure, you can find him writing about them on his blog http://doubletroubledaddy.com.*

THE SINK

Francis Linardo, Knoxville, TN

One of the first things any good golf teacher will tell you is "develop a routine." Get a pre-shot ritual and do it the same way every time. The theory being, consistency breeds success. The more you do it, the more you're comfortable doing it. If things start to fall apart, your routine is there to fall back on to steady the ship. I am not consistent with my pre-shot routine, which is one of the myriad reasons I am no good at golf. But this is one of those areas where golf has a life lesson to teach. I'm referring to our time in the Neonatal Intensive Care Unit at the University of Tennessee Medical Center.

It gets pretty crazy in there as you might imagine. The first time you see it is on the mandatory tour before the birth of your child, or in our case, children. They poured Tracy into a wheel chair and we rolled over from her hospital room where she had been on bed-rest for about three weeks, across the hall to the Neonatal Intensive Care Unit or NICU, pronounced "Nick U." It might as well get certified as its own University, it has been a college-level education every minute we've been in there.

After rolling through the secured double doors, the first thing you see that requires your attention is The Sink; two of them actually: the silent sentinels of the NICU. If you don't visit The Sink and pay the proper homage, your journey ends, immediately.

No place can be completely germ free, but the NICU has to be as germ free as possible because the little babies who couldn't wait the full forty weeks, left behind their coat of immunity on their dash to freedom. If you want admittance to a true Magic Kingdom, you must appease The Sink.

Here's how it works: you go to The Sink, step on the two pedals on the floor to start the water, bare your arms to your elbows (although I have learned that if you want your sleeves to be dry at the cuffs you need to push them well past your elbow), get your arms wet from elbow to fingertip and start soaping. If there is a chance you still have some pulled pork or curly fry remains under your fingernails, there is a cup with what I call miniature Punji Sticks, but is conveniently marked "Finger Nail Cleaners." Let's just say, if the NICU is ever attacked or a particular doctor is not giving me the info I want, that cup will come in handy. Dull they ain't.

After sufficient soaping of the hands and arms from the fingertips up to and including the elbows, you rinse, completely. Then repeat. And then again, until you have done this for three minutes.

After the three minutes is up, you dry completely. No medical reason for this, just function. If your hands are a little wet, the next step is not pleasant. After washing and drying, you apply an alcohol-based sanitizer to your hands. The sanitizer is so strong it takes several minutes to get it rubbed in to a point that will allow you to separate your fingers. If your hands are even a little moist, you can forget doing anything but Spock's "Live Long and Prosper" gesture for at least an hour. I'm talking about the real Spock now, Science Officer of the Enterprise, not that fake Dr. dude who wrote all those ludicrous children's books.

Once the sanitizer is applied, your identity has been transformed. You are now recognized as a welcomed member of the NICU and are free to pretty much wander and do as you please.

Tracy is a rule follower. She followed this procedure without complaint because she was afraid of getting in trouble and didn't want to be accused of bringing in a microbe that might wipe out the entire preemie population. My three-minute commitment was much deeper.

The Sink, once viewed as a three-minute burden that felt more like an hour, became a safe haven for me, much like the pre-shot routine is supposed to offer to my golf swing. Things can get crazy in the NICU and over a three-week period in June, they were probably at their craziest. Babies we came to know passed away, others clung to life. Anne Marie, on two separate occasions over those weeks, had such major setbacks we thought it was the end of the line. We thought we would be burying her right next to her sister Linda Claire, who we had buried not three months prior. When things appear to be falling apart, you need something to anchor to; something routine, something you know won't be different as all other circumstances change at a blinding pace.

The Sink was consistent. I knew what to do when I got there, doing it everyday for five months. It gave me three minutes to gather whatever mental clarity I may need to make decisions for Anne Marie when I got to her room, after having to walk past other rooms where other babies were fighting the fight and other parents were making life and death decisions.

When a call comes early in the morning and a doctor is on the line, you know it's not good. The normal crazy will be ramped up on your visit that day.

There may be a new nurse in your baby's room; your uneasiness starts to rise. No matter that she is the best at what she does, highly trained, abundantly qualified in technical and personal skill and will probably save the life of a baby that very day; maybe your baby. She is new to you.

There are ten doctors in the group of physicians that handle the NICU. Today might be the day you meet a Doc you've never seen before, anxiety comes now. Will she change the medication or feeding plan? Who knows? All these things occurred on a daily basis, each one knocking you off your pins just a little bit more than the last thing did.

But The Sink, The Sink became invaluable. The Sink never changed, the routine never changed. There was solid ground there. It really was the only solid ground in the place.

My hands have never been cleaner.

***Francis Linardo**, originally born and raised in Mays Landing, NJ with his five sisters and two brothers, now lives in Knoxville TN with his wife Tracy, son Frank and daughter Anne Marie. He retired from the United States Air Force in 2009 to be a stay-at-home dad. Find more of his writing at www.franknfran.com.*

PART THREE

BUILT DAD TOUGH

"I informed the lady I do teach my kids to share and also teach them to wait their turn if someone is playing with a toy they want. She gets mad, tells me, 'This is why men should not raise kids.'"
- *Nick Withington, father of two from Overland Park, KS*

A MAN'S PLACE

Christopher T. VanDijk, Denver, CO

My life is pretty easy and pretty boring.

I'm the stay-at-home dad to "Turtle" my five-year-old son. We live in a new home in one of the most beautiful states in the country, Colorado. My wife loves me (most of the time). Summers are not too hot. Winters are not too cold. I occasionally get to act and write which are my passions beyond kissing my wife and making my boy giggle.

However, once in awhile, I am smacked in the face by the fact that some people have a problem with my decision to be the primary caregiver, instead of leaving that duty to my wife or a childcare center.

The other day I took Turtle to the playground. I hadn't heard enough of his giggles yet that day. There was a new dad on the playground. He looked like my kind of dude: vaguely hipstery (skinny jeans, beard, hipster hair cut, requisite cup of coffee). He was engaged with his four kids, having a great time on the playground and chatting with the other parents. After some small talk about our kids, he asked what I did for a living. I told him, "I'm a stay-at-home dad."

He knit his eyebrows and gave me a sidelong glance, "Really?"

"Yes."

He shook his head a little as I began prepping for the typical questions.

"When did you lose your job?"

"I didn't," I replied. "My wife has always made more than me and it just made sense for our family."

He stared at me for a second and said, "I'm sorry. I think I might have the answer for you."

"The answer to what?"

"I think I can help you get your balls back."

I was so caught off guard that I didn't have a reaction. I was just blank. He began telling me about the new church he and another guy started in our community recreation center. He moved from California to "plant" it here. He then started quoting scripture about men's and women's places in the family and hierarchies and such. He had a name for it and asked, "Have you ever watched the Duggar family? On television? They're big in the movement."

"I think I'll pass," I stammered in utter disbelief.

Then he called me a lost soul and said he'd pray for me.

I was floored.

Totally. Floored.

I've been asked if I am "babysitting the kids for mommy today?" (No, dads don't babysit their own kids) but I've never been called "a lost soul" because I decided to raise my own kid.

Unbelievably, it got worse.

The next morning my wife shared a flier on our community's Facebook page with a "WTF?"

It was posted by the guy I met the day before, inviting men to an all day gun outing of "Men doing what men should do. Shoot stuff." The church he "planted" here sponsored it. Their letterhead said, "Simply Jesus" on the top.

"Would 'simply Jesus' choose a simple shotgun or simple semi-automatic?" I deadpanned in my own head.

I was disturbed on many levels. First, the event was all day on a Saturday, when most men who do work outside the home would have time to spend with their families. Second, I thought it was ridiculous to need to shoot something to make a man feel more masculine. How about hugging your kid? That's pretty manly in my book. Third, I have a hard time believing Jesus would rather our family struggle on whatever income I could earn rather than live more comfortably from the much higher income my wife is capable of earning.

Perhaps, most disturbing though, was the paradigm this father had set up for how he felt my son should be raised; that what I offered by way of teaching him compassion, courage, joy, and a sense of self-worth were lacking because I, as a father, did not somehow meet his standard of manliness.

I thought society was realizing men are equally capable caregivers who enjoy being with their kids. Apparently, some people still subscribe to old stereotypes.

I'm not going to worry about them too much, though. I have a giggle quota to fill today.

Christopher T. VanDijk *is an actor, writer, dad, and firefighter. Chris is an award-winning screenwriter and actor, contributor to the Huffington Post and you can find him raising cain online at his blog, http://SkinnedKneesInShortPants.blogspot.com/. Chris is also the facilitator of the Denver Dad's Group and a volunteer firefighter with the South Adams County Fire Department. He can usually be found in local Denver parks chasing a toddler, digging for dinosaur bones, and discussing everything from politics to pasta. One of his stories also appeared in* Dads Behaving DADLY: 67 Truths, Tears and Triumphs of Modern Fatherhood.

THE OVER-PROTECTOR

Christopher Sansone, Pleasant Hill, CA

Every year, during the second week of July, my folks spend a week in Lake Tahoe along the north shore in King's Beach. This was our second year attending with our kids and we were excited our 20-month-old James was old enough to appreciate the water (which he loves, thanks to his mother's genes) and to bring Alexander, our most recent addition, on his first trip to the beach. The week was great and the kids had a blast. On Saturday we were all in a good mood but tired as we headed home on our three-hour drive.

Although our car was capable of making it home on one tank of gas, we knew traveling with a 20-month old and five-month-old meant we were going to make at least one stop, whether we liked it or not.

Somewhere outside of Sacramento, James needed to stretch his legs and Alexander needed to nurse. There was no waiting; no cherry-picking our stop. They wanted what they wanted RIGHT NOW!

I pulled in to the parking lot of the first fast food joint off the freeway. Our parking spot faced a busy street that served as the main artery for traffic to get on and off the highway and was right behind a bus stop. It was not ideal for nursing, but I've learned that a mother's modesty kind of goes out the window with the second kid.

As soon as I got out of the car to hopefully make this our only stop, a woman at the bus stop hollered and asked me for fifty cents. She was a robust woman, probably in her mid-40's, but looked much older due to some hard living, I imagined. Not a transient, but she certainly was not living comfortably.

I immediately told her no, without thinking. I wasn't in the mood for panhandlers, considering all the things I had to do. My answer was quickly met with a scowl and some unintelligible muttering. I didn't care.

Normally I'm more polite with panhandlers, but I just wanted to get the kids fed, changed and back on the road. I had no patience for her.

It was at that point my focus pulled back from the family tasks at hand and I started to take in my surroundings. I realized we were in a bit of a dicey area.

For the last sixteen years I have been a cop. When I say "dicey area," I know what I'm talking about. When I say I can recognize predatory, opportunist behavior, it's because I've seen it. When you hear me speak about assessing people as a physical threat or not, it's because I've had years of training and experience.

Instantly I switched to work mode. I was not happy about it; I go on vacation to get out of this mindset. My instinct was to stay with the car and act as sentry while my wife took care of the boys, but the family workflow and a desire to get home required us to perform different tasks at the same time.

As I went about completing what needed to be done, which included going into the restaurant to get food for my wife and James, I was keenly focused on this woman because something about her did not sit right with me. I watched her from inside the restaurant while waiting for our food. I noticed she was uninterested in the bus that just arrived. She then drifted away from the bus stop, wandering into the parking lot with no purpose to her movement, constantly looking around.

I identified her as a predator.

Not in the "It puts the lotion on its skin" guy from Silence of the Lambs type of predator. More in the opportunistic "Oh, I see you left your garage door open so thanks for the power tools" type.

I returned to the car, got James situated with some food in the driver's seat, and my wife handed me Alexander to change his diaper so she could eat. I started toward the trashcan to dispose of the diaper, which was across the parking lot at the restaurant entrance, and saw her continuing to drift through the lot.

I dropped the diaper in the bin, turned back towards the car and realized she was now heading back toward the bus stop on a trajectory that would take her right past the driver's side of my car. I became laser focused on her, about twenty-five feet behind.

As she walked by, I saw her head turn toward the driver's window where my 20-month-old son was sitting, pretending to drive. She stopped, turning her body toward my car.

And that was when I lost my mind.

I closed the gap between us quickly – not running – but moving with purpose. I crossed the threshold of the rear bumper and told her, in no uncertain terms and with forcefulness rarely necessary outside of work, "Get the f*ck away from my car!"

A look of fear washed over her face. She recoiled and began stammering out an apology as she backed toward the sanctuary of the bus stop without taking her eyes off me. Her reaction told me she saw violence behind my eyes and, although I had no intention of visiting violence upon her, it was there.

The last bit of family business before we were back on the road was to buckle the boys back in their car seats and for the missus to use the restroom. As I sat in the car waiting, I began to second-guess my behavior and actions.

Looking through this relatively new lens of fatherhood, I had seen her as a threat, whether real or perceived, to my children. My reaction was not born from cognitive thought; it was an instinctive response.

I felt horrible, like a bully. I knew, and still know, there was nothing wrong with how I reacted even though it was likely she had no ill intentions. I have no doubt even the most mild-mannered parents would aggressively protect their children. However, I believe this instinctive response, coupled with my career experience, caused my reaction to come more swiftly than it would have with others.

When my wife returned to the car, I got out and approached the woman at the bus stop. "I'm sorry I talked to you like that back there," I said. "I don't know you and I didn't know your intentions which is why I reacted the way I did. I hope you understand it wasn't personal, I'm just very protective of my family."

"I understand," she replied. "You were just looking out for you babies."

She was right; I was. We shook hands and I took my babies home.

Instincts are powerful. This was the first time I had experienced such a profound instinctive response that was not centered on me. I'm a dad now, cognitively and instinctively. And, in both ways, I am and will continue to be overprotective.

***Christopher Sansone** is a 40-year-old husband and father of two boys under the age of 2 who lives in the San Francisco Bay Area. When he's not balancing his hectic shift-work schedule in law enforcement, he is spending as much time as he can with his boys. More of his writing can be found at www.ThePArentalShift.com.*

PURSUING THE DREAM

Adam Hall, Burlington, VT

I used to be an opera singer. That is a difficult thing for me to write because I spent so many years, and much more money, in my attempts to succeed in the complicated world of opera. My hard work and money were paying off, though. I received contracts with the New York City Opera and The Metropolitan Opera.

When my children were born, I knew there were sacrifices all of us would have to make for me to continue following my dream. I was determined to be both an involved parent and a successful singer. Choosing one over the other seemed unnecessary.

The longest I ever left my family was for two months. I was offered a spot to train in a prestigious program with a world-renowned singer, but it was on the other side of the country, which meant not seeing my family for over eight weeks. Tears streamed down my face as I walked away from them at the airport. I didn't want to be away from them for one day, so two months felt like an eternity. Despite my sadness, I was sure I was making the right decision. I knew once I was more established, I would be able to bring them with me. They would travel the world with me! I would talk to them everyday. Technology would keep us close. It would all be worth it. At least, that's what my brain was telling me, even though I was getting conflicting information from my heart.

A day in October, however, pushed what I was feeling in my heart straight to my brain. We were spending a pleasant afternoon at a friend's farm when I saw my daughter lying on the ground, motionless. I called her name. She didn't answer. She had been diagnosed with epilepsy in the spring, but her symptoms had disappeared with medication and she had not had any episodes for months. My wife ran over to check on her, and then screamed for me to come. I have never run so hard in my life. My five-year-old daughter was breathing, but completely catatonic. I scooped her up into my arms and we raced to the hospital as she remained totally out of it for almost 45 minutes.

The doctors could not tell us anything. This wasn't like the normal seizures they had seen. It lasted nearly an hour and was without convulsions. It didn't fit within any of their models. The best they could do was suggest we switch medications and hope it didn't happen again.

On Halloween weekend, I left my family again to spend a few days auditioning for several opera houses in New York City. I was elated, for I was sure I had nailed the auditions and would get a call back. On my return home, I received a call from my wife telling me it had happened again. The catatonic seizure lasted even longer this time and she told me to meet them at the hospital as soon as I could. Speed limits be damned, I raced to the emergency room to be with my family, sick to my stomach the whole time.

"How could I have left them?!" I shouted at myself. They needed me, and I wasn't there. I was off pursuing a dream that suddenly, no matter how I tried to spin it, seemed very selfish. As we switched medications yet again, my whole world seemed ready to collapse at the slightest provocation. What should I do? Was it possible to be a good father and a traveling singer at the same time? Would staying home make a difference? Was there even anything at all I could do? With these questions heavy on my heart, I continued on my life path, trudging a little slower.

When my agent sent word of another audition that winter, I agreed to it, and made arrangements to drop off my daughter and her two-year-old brother at my mother's house for the weekend. My children were both very excited to spend some time at Grammy's, but something was off for me. About thirty minutes into the drive, I suddenly hit the brakes on my car and pulled over to the side of the highway. I turned on my hazard lights and rested my head on the steering wheel.

"What's wrong, Daddy?" my kids asked from the backseat. I couldn't tell them. I couldn't even tell myself. All I knew was I wanted to go home. I had never had such a strong feeling in my life. I NEEDED to go home. Turning around, I told my children we were going home. "Noooo! Waaaaah! We want to go to GRAMMY'S!" they complained. I turned back around and headed to my mother's because a trip promised to Grammy's is a trip always granted.

When I got to my mother's, I called my agent, my voice teacher and my best friends. I needed advice. I needed to know if I was freaking out for no reason or if this was a legitimate existential crisis. All I knew was that I would not be able to live with myself if something happened to one of my children when I was not around. And even if nothing catastrophic happened, I came to realize the missed baseball games, dance recitals, concerts, birthdays, and bedtimes were no longer worth it. I asked my agent not to schedule more auditions. My voice teacher told me not to worry because I could always come back to it when the kids were older. Maybe I will.

The one person I hesitated to call was my wife. The thought of facing her, after all she had sacrificed to put me through grad school, support the family, and raise the kids alone while I was traveling, was terrifying. I felt ashamed. I felt like a failure. I felt as if I had given up on something we had both become heavily invested in. But she was very supportive, as she has always been, and I think she likes having me around more.

I still sing locally. I teach voice lessons, conduct a church choir, and write about music and parenting. But mostly I spend time with my family, trying to put my kids' needs first.

And I used to be an opera singer.

***Adam Hall** is a father, writer, and classically trained musician. He is a stay-at-home dad who lives in Vermont with his wife and two children while writing regularly at www.tenordad.com.*

ALL I EVER WANTED

Jason Grant, Riverdale, NY

It was 2 a.m. the morning after my son Jake was born when the doctors insisted I go home and get some rest. It was bitter cold and snowing outside as I hailed a cab. Inside, I felt warm and grateful this would be the last time I returned to an empty apartment. Strangely, I didn't feel tired and had no desire to sleep. I just wanted to soak in the joy I was experiencing as a new father and my good fortune in having seen my son come into the world. I set the alarm to wake me at 6 a.m. in case I fell asleep. I wanted to be at Lori and Jake's bedside as soon as visiting hours resumed. Lying in bed with my clothes still on, I drifted off for two hours of restless sleep. I kept playing the memory of Jake's birth on a loop. When the alarm woke me up, I was energized with the knowledge I would be back with my family to create even more memories to cherish.

That was four years ago. I don't want to miss a moment with him, yet I often catch myself wishing he were older. The way young girls plan their wedding day years in advance, I have been planning my son's childhood. There are things I want to teach him and pass down to him. I envision him playing in little league. I see myself teaching him how to write and play with friends and grow from a good boy into an even better man. I can't wait!

Lori often has to remind me to stop dreaming because, someday, sooner than I can ever expect, he WILL be older. Jake will likely have other things on his mind than spending time with his old man. That is why I am so grateful to have been given the chance to raise him full-time, without many of the "conventional" career responsibilities.

To be honest, never in my life did I see myself becoming a stay-at-home dad. I fell into this job because I was in the process of shifting careers when Lori went back to work. We both knew I had to step up to the plate. While it is not an easy job, physically or emotionally, I don't see it as a burden. Being Jake's daddy is the best job I've ever had.

There is so much Jake has given me and so much I hope I am giving him. Every day we spend together, I find I am learning and becoming a better man. He has given me the incentive to improve as a human being. I am trying to be more realistic and responsible and I am slowly learning to let negativity roll off my back. I have always been easily frustrated, so I have to remind myself to "catch and release" when tension takes hold of my body. I am trying to get better at taking suggestions from others who have been through this process already. My outlook on life and parenthood has changed dramatically over the last four years.

I remain thankful for being able to experience the things Jake can do and has already done. I am amazed at his intellect. At the age of three, he was able to play and solve the memory game on my wife's cell phone in under two minutes. He can already read and can even give us accurate directions when we are on the highway. It's as if he has a GPS inside his own little head. I am now less obsessed with my own fatherly fantasies. Jake's dreams and plans for his life are more important to me than my plans for him.

I know the day will come when Jake will be a grown man and he will have a life of his own. I wonder how much of his childhood he will remember. He certainly won't remember the moment he was born. He probably won't remember taking his first steps or speaking his first words or singing "I had a little dreidel" for the first time. He might remember how cute and adorable he looked dressed up for Halloween as Yoda and as Chewbacca or, more recently, in his little knight of the crusades costume, although that will mostly be from photographs. He probably won't remember how, every day for three years, I would wake him up from his nap and stand him in his crib with his arms stretched out. I would lift him up and he would wrap his arms around my neck, hugging me so tightly. But I will remember.

I will remember everything, especially the joy, the pride and, yes, the frustration all parents experience when raising their children. Mostly, I will remember my love for him and that he is all I ever wanted.

Jason Grant *is a full-time dad, a contributing blogger for the NYC Dads Group, and a professional writer who spreads awareness of Tourette syndrome and its related disorders. By far, the best and most challenging job Jason has ever held is being Jake's Daddy. You can read more about them at http://www.daddylogue.com/.*

HANDICAPING FATHERHOOD

Paul Gilbride, Chesterfield, MO

I have been an at-home-dad for twelve years. If I had to draw an analogy about what it has been like, I would describe it as my own personal submission into a witness protection program. The change in identity is profound, and similar to the witness protection program, it is like beginning a whole new life (minus the looking over your shoulder for someone who wants to kill you part).

My personal identity crises began early in my tenure as an at-home dad. As the old saying goes, sink or swim, and I learned to swim thanks to a weekend golf outing that, to everyone else, was an escape from who they normally were, but for me, turned out to be an awakening into who I could be.

I was roughly two months into my stint as an at-home-dad. My son Calvin was five and had started kindergarten that September. My daughter Molly, who was three, was clearly capable of starting kindergarten as well, even though she was still two years away. Since the kids were both still alive, my experiment as an at-home dad had met our primary success criteria. My reward for a successful two months of work was a weekend golf outing with fifteen other guys. Already burdened by a 26 handicap, I now had to lug into this weekend the explanation of why I was now a stay-at-home dad.

My fifteen cohorts for the weekend were successful professionals, ranging from an executive for an investment company to a head chef at one of downtown's best restaurants. I was now a recovering CPA, changing diapers and taking names.

Loaded with anxiety, I packed my clubs, about five dozen balls (26 handicap, remember) and a suitcase filled with clothes to prepare me for anything from freezing rain to 50's and sunny. It was October in Minnesota, anything could happen, and usually did. Last minute preparations included a half hour of instructions about the kids' schedule with my wife, Nancy. In hindsight, I did not treat this with the care and detail I should have. After all, I was the idiot dad handing the kids over to their mother. It was clearly a step up for them, right?

I arrived at my destination about mid-morning on a Thursday. We all met at the golf course to play a practice round which would be used for a draft that evening.

Things actually went pretty smoothly. I golfed with two guys I knew and who knew my "situation," so I could focus more on how terrible of a golfer I was instead of worrying about how much of a loser they might think I was. That evening we focused on beer, scotch, cigars, good food and the 16-man draft. The subject of what I did for a living never came up. I went to bed that night with my "shameful secret" in tact. The next day, however, would prove to be a different story.

The golf course parking lot was buzzing the following morning. As I put on my shoes, I saw several of the guys break off by themselves, some with phones balanced between their cheek and shoulder as they walked, others with Bluetooth devices. All were pacing the parking lot, undoubtedly getting their offices prepared for their absences that day. I grabbed my phone and threw it in my bag. I was not expecting any calls from the office or any clients, but not having a phone might certainly give away my perceived relative unimportance.

Right around the completion of the third hole, I noticed guys pulling out phones, mostly listening to messages, some getting in a quick call as we drove between holes. In what was probably an effort to fit in or just because there was no one to talk to, I grabbed my phone out of my bag. It was only about 8:00 in the morning and I was not sure exactly who I thought would be calling me this early. Unbelievably, I had a message:

Hello Mr. Gilbride, this is Mrs. Cramdilly from the Prior Lake school district. One of our bus drivers has your son on her bus at Five Hawks Elementary School. It appears that your son got on the wrong bus. Can you please call me back as soon as possible? Thank you.

The first thing I muttered to myself was something along the lines of, "Holy Sh*t, are you kidding me?" How the hell does a five year old get on the wrong bus?

The guys were now getting ready to tee off at the next hole. I gave them a wave and told them I would be right there. I immediately called Mrs. Cramdilly. "Oh, hi Mr. Gilbride. We figured out that Calvin goes to St. Michael's and he is on his way there now."

"How did this happen?" I asked out of disbelief.

"Well, Betty is a substitute driver and this was her first time on this route. She did not realize Calvin was on the wrong bus until she finished her route."

Okay that made sense. I thanked her and asked for a call when Calvin was at his school, safe and sound.

I put away my phone and hurried to the tee box where the others in my group were waiting. One guy noticed the serious look on my face and asked if "things were blowing up at the office." "I guess you could say that," I replied, and went back to playing golf. Could my wife have been so careless as to put him on the wrong bus? I wondered. I was sure I gave her the bus number before I left.

Minutes later I did get a call from my son's school, letting me know he had arrived safe and sound. I tried calling my wife, no answer.

"Wow, you really can't get away. What is it you do for a living?" asked my golfing partner. Taken completely off guard, and consequently with very little thought about how anxious I had been about answering this question no more than an hour ago, I replied, "Believe it or not, I stay at home with my kids. And believe it or not, my wife put my kindergarten son on the wrong bus this morning."

I think my response caught him equally off guard. After a brief silence he said, "Wow, good for you, I could never do that. So your wife put him on the wrong bus? That sounds like something I would do."

In between the front and back nine I finally got a call from my wife. She indeed had been unaware that Calvin was on the wrong bus. Since all had ended well, we laughed it off.

Later, somewhere on the back nine, my phone rang again. This time we were in between holes and I picked up.

"Hello, Mr. Gilbride. This is Mrs. Cramdilly from the Prior Lake School district. Our bus is parked outside your house with your son Calvin and no one is home. Are you in the area?"

No I was not in the area, I was about 200 miles away. Where the hell is my wife?! I screamed into my head.

"Let me call you right back Mrs. Cramdilly, I will try to reach my wife."

Luckily I reached Nancy on the first ring.

"Hi honey, how's the golf going?" she happily asked.

"Where the hell are you?" I replied, with a less than equally happy tone.

"I'm about five minutes away from home. Molly and I were at Nordstrom's doing a little shopping."

"I told you Calvin gets dropped off at 12:45!" I scolded. "The bus is sitting there waiting for you."

"Oh crap, what time is it?"

"I'm not sure." I replied, "but they are waiting so please hurry up." I hung up.

I called Mrs. Cramdilly and let her know my wife would be there soon. Luckily Calvin was the last to be dropped off, so the bus driver waited. Again, when all was said and done, he got home safe and all was well.

I returned to the group as they were teeing off on the next hole. I am sure from the look on my face as I paced around the tee box, talking on the phone, they must have all figured I had either closed or lost some huge corporate merger. My partner knew better, so I just walked up to the tee and threw my wife under the bus (no pun intended) and explained what happened.

The topic did not come up for the rest of the round. We lost, and I golfed like crap. Everything seemed to be back to normal.

I learned some valuable lessons that weekend I still carry with me today. I learned that, despite being a man, I am every bit as capable, if not more so, of taking care of my kids. I also learned that women are not necessarily instinctual caregivers. They learn on the job, just like men. I also learned that I am not defined by what I do but by why I do it. I left corporate America to take on a job that had more meaning for me. I also learned my golfing buddies respected me, not as much because I chose to be the primary caregiver, but because I did it without having to apologize for it.

Since that weekend I never saw myself as anything other than a man who made a particular life choice. In addition, my wife and I never saw our family situation as a role reversal, but simply as a team who's roles were equally significant to establishing a healthy, happy family.

Stereotypes can be smashed, and when they are, they pave the way for a new and better way of life.

***Paul Gilbride** is a recovering CPA turned stay-at-home dad. After fifteen years in corporate America, Paul moved into the role of Domestic CEO for the Gilbride Family, which includes wife Nancy, son Calvin, daughter Molly and Otis and Bucky the dogs. Paul has been at home for 12 years and now runs Trickle Down Happiness, LLC, a coaching practice dedicated to making good stay-at-home dads, great stay-at-home dads.*

PERSEVERANCE

Adam Rust, Covington, KY

In the words of the eccentric 1970's rock band, *Queen*, I like to ride my bicycle!

I also enjoy camping in the woods.

Most of all, I love to spend time with my children.

When I can put these three things together, I get my absolute favorite thing: riding my bicycle with my children to a place where we camp in the woods. I call it "bike camping with kids" or "bi-ca-wi-ki" for short.

The winter of 2014 was harsh in the Midwest. I spent most of it daydreaming about the first day it would be warm enough to load our camping gear on the bike and hit the road for a weekend of bicawiki.

I checked the weather forecast, week after frozen week. Thoughts of road kill, campfires and singing songs with my kids while pedaling were the only things keeping me sane as I waited to embark on the first bicawiki trip of the year.

The weather forecast for the second weekend in April was looking good – temperatures in the 40s and no rain. It wasn't optimal bicawiki weather, but close enough. My seven-year old daughter was the only family member who accepted my invitation.

Saturday finally arrived. I attached her tag-along bike to my bike so our two bikes became one, much like a semi-truck attaches to its cargo trailer. We loaded the food and camping gear onto our human-powered road rig and set off into the brisk morning air. Leaf buds were on the tree limbs. Birds were chirping. The sun was bright in the sky. It seemed like the perfect conditions for riding the twenty-five miles to our friend's property where we planned to camp.

We were both grinning ear to ear as we hit the road. I felt like I could pedal all day long. But four miles into the ride, my daughter's joy faded and gave way to complaint.

"Daddy, I'm cold. I need to stop."

We pulled over to the side of the road to assess the situation. Tears began flowing down her cheeks and she demanded we return home. The fruit of my loins was staging mutiny on the USS Bikecamper over a few goose bumps. I knew she could handle this ride because she has done more difficult rides than this before. I paused to consider my response.

The macho man in me wanted to tell her to suck it up, challenge her to push on and continue on to camp. I certainly did not want to consider retreat as an option. In a moment of fatherly clarity, I decided to exercise some patience and attend to her needs before making a decision about the trip's fate. Her need was simple: She was cold. I dug a warm coat out of our cargo bag and wrapped her up in it. Then I wrapped her up in my embrace and waited for the sobbing to stop.

We enjoyed a snack together, and I told her she would certainly get warmer as we pedaled up the next hill, especially if she kept the coat on. I asked her if she thought she could press on. She quietly nodded her head. I replied with a smile to let the silence linger a bit longer.

She broke the silence with a question that seemed to come from nowhere.

"Daddy, what's a motto?"

"It's a short little saying that expresses an idea about how a person wants to live their life. Do you remember Dori from Finding Nemo? Her motto was, 'Just keep swimming.'"

"Oh, I see. I think I know my new motto: Always persevere."

"That's a great motto! I see that you are living by your motto right now. You're going to persevere on this trip, aren't you?"

"Yeah! Just keep pedaling!"

I gave her a big hug. My heart overflowed with joy. My daughter was learning a valuable lesson about dedication and persistence. Minutes before she had been a sobbing mess, wanting to return to the warmth and comfort of home. Now she was determined to continue our father-daughter adventure and become the poster child for perseverance. We got back on the bikes and pedaled the remaining miles to our campsite with lighthearted chatting and laughing all the way.

After we settled in at the campsite, we lit a fire, ate dinner and snuggled into our cozy tent. Several hours later, I woke up to tend the fire. The quiet of the pre-dawn hour provided me with time for reflection on the moment we had shared.

I thought about how tragically the situation could have ended if I had reacted defensively to my daughter's emotions and pressured her to bike on. She would have dug her heels in further, cried more and rebelled harder. Patience proved to be a better strategy. By demonstrating to her that I understood her need and would take care of her, I created a safe place for her to choose perseverance for herself.

This experience was a good lesson for my daughter about how she can persevere through adversity, especially when supported by her father. It also taught me a good lesson about the importance of listening to my children and demonstrating concern for their well-being. As I do, the trust I build with her allows us to go places together we never thought possible.

***Adam Rust** is husband to his wonderful wife and father to his five amazing, fun, and thoroughly interesting children. Adam once thought he never wanted be a father. Now, he finds his greatest joy in life in the everyday moments of fatherhood. By day, he works at a video production company called Epipheo. By night, he shares his reflections on fatherhood at www.fathervision.com. He is also chief content curator at www.dailyedify.com.*

LOOKING GOOD, DAD

Richard Blake, Lafayette, CO

I was speechless. This father, who I had met only seconds ago at my son Eliot's opening day of soccer practice, had caught me so off guard that I was unable to form a response.

The conversation had begun quite innocently. After a late arrival on our recreation center's multipurpose field, I had just completed the usual set-up routine (picnic blanket, child blanket, umbrella, snacks, water, milk, toys, and changing bag) and was settling into forty-five minutes of cheering, alongside my two-year-old daughter, the flailing mass of feet and legs that was my son's Pee Wee soccer practice. While the players were still huddled with their coaches, I took a moment to scan the sidelines. Amid the usual clusters of moms, nannies, grandmothers, and siblings I had come to know over the last year were two men sitting back in folding canvas recliners complete with umbrellas, cup holders, coolers and foot rests.

It was hard to contain my excitement. Could these also be stay-at-home dads? I wondered. It was way too early for most working parents to be there. I gathered up Eliot's sister, Corinne, along with a milk Sippy, a blanket, and a couple of toys and headed over to the men's sport-watching oasis.

"Hi!" I said. "How are you guys?" I expertly tossed the blanket onto the ground, not even watching as it unfurled into a flat pad, then lowered my daughter onto it. Without breaking eye contact with the men, I opened my right arm and let the milk Sippy I had been holding in the crook of my elbow roll down my forearm and land squarely in my daughter's groping hand. I waited for their responses to my question and my stunning display of fatherhood dexterity.

"Hi," the men said back in a friendly way, but without offering to extend the conversation. Faltering a bit, I pulled out the tried-and-true question I ask whenever I see a man out with a child at a park or grocery store during normal, working hours, "Are either of you at-home dads?"

The friend of the first man (who I will call Father B) clucked his tongue and let out a wistful, "Man, I wish!" His tone was not that of someone familiar with full time childcare and home management. Rather, it was the idyllic intonations of someone who believed taking care of children was more like babysitting than a full engagement of all of your faculties and that managing a house amounted to an occasional toilet cleaning and rinsing out of your own drinking glass for someone else to wash later.

Father A, the first man, answered my query with a simple "Nope."

"I'm a full-time, at-home dad," I said with a sort of understated pride, "Five years of service!" I then added, "I am always looking to meet other dads who either take care of their kids full time or who otherwise spend a lot of time with them."

"Really?" said Father A. "You stay home all of the time? Does that mean you do the housework, too?"

"Yep," I replied, perhaps now overstating my pride. "I do the cooking, washing, cleaning, well, you name it! If it happens in the house or with the kids, I do it."

After considering my words, Father A began his response with, "Wow, better not let the ladies find out about that …" As he paused, my mind completed his sentences with the common phrases I've heard before, such as "… then the ladies will expect that from all of us" or "… it will make it tough on the rest of us." Instead, Father A continued with, "…because if the ladies learn about what you do, they won't find you very attractive."

I was stunned. I was utterly speechless. As time moved excruciatingly slow, I carefully considered the appropriate response. In my five years of full-time fatherhood I had heard quite a few odd questions and even outright assertions about my manhood, masculinity, and mental state. "So, you're gay, then?" asked a woman at a mall play area. "When did you lose your job? Are you still looking for work?" wondered both women and men at the park. "Are you disabled?" inquired a nanny. "I guess we know who rules YOUR roost!" declared a former truck driver turned landscaper. "You must be crazy," asserted a self-proclaimed business wiz. "I'm sorry, I hope things get better for you," sympathized a homeless man after he inquired about my work as a prelude to asking for money.

While I am very proud of my role as a stay-at-home dad, I have had my own doubts about my career viability, mental capacity, masculinity and net societal worth. In middle school, I learned how others perceived my worth as a person after being knocked unconscious by a kid during recess, dragged across the crowded gym floor, and then stuffed behind a set of bleachers without anyone saying a word or ultimately being held accountable.

Months later, my attractiveness and desirability to women garnered a less than affirming value when the first girl I had ever asked out (to the middle school Valentine's Day Dance, no less) apparently experienced a breakdown afterwards. A friend reported that she had arrived to her next period class in a panic, exclaiming "Why me, why me, oh God, why me."

For much of my life I had struggled with my identity, and at this moment, Father A was tapping into my insecurities like they were an over-pressurized keg.

Then, a woman sitting near us who, evidently, had been paying close attention to our conversation, remarked, "Well, I would find that attractive."

There was an edge of assertiveness in her voice as she made direct eye contact with Father A, almost daring a response. Father A answered her challenge with a dismissive, "I guess that's why we're not married anymore."

"Damn right!" said the woman, turning away triumphantly. I smiled and turned my attention to more important matters - the practice. "Go Eliot!" I shouted. "Go Eliot!" mimicked Corinne. "Go Eliot!" echoed the woman, and then added with a smile, "And way to go at-home dad!"

***Richard Blake**, a child since birth, provides full time care for two amazing kids and part time frustration for a wonderful wife at his centrally located*

Colorado home. Prior to his current role as master of his domestic domain, Richard held highly skilled but entirely unappreciated positions in academia and corporate America. Brain care specialist Gag Halfrunt had this addition to Mr. Blake's biography: „Vell, Richard's just zis guy, you know?"

MY CAR CAUGHT ON FIRE

Creed Anthony, Indianapolis, IN

My daughter started kindergarten last year, which brought a host of fears – How would she adjust? Would she make friends? Would she eat lunch in the cafeteria? Would she be safe on the bus?

My car wasn't one of those fears.

The fire happened on the first day of the second week of school – the first Monday of the school year. It was 6:30 a.m.

The freeway is two minutes from our home. I had just pulled onto the on-ramp when I noticed a car right on my tail. I hit the gas, hoping that accelerating would distance myself from the other driver and, perhaps, give him an opportunity to pass me as the freeway opened to three lanes.

My car did not accelerate.

The car angrily swerved from behind me. The guy was now parallel to my car. I didn't want to look at him (you can't give a road rager an audience) so I kept my gaze ahead, focusing on the road, ignoring him. I pressed the gas again.

My car still wouldn't accelerate.

What the heck?

My daughter was singing along to Radio Disney, a morning ritual, oblivious to the potential conflict in the next lane. The man was now honking his horn; his window down.

And he was shouting.

Apprehensively, I rolled my window down to hear what he was saying. I was slightly concerned my car would not accelerate but I didn't know if this guy was trying to tell me I had a flat or something or if he was going to try to "correct" my driving.

Leaning across the empty passenger seat of his Jeep to project his voice through the howling wind on the freeway, he yelled at me, "Dude! Your car is on fire!"

I gave him a quizzical look.

"Your CAR," he yelled again, "is on FIRE!!!"

This was not something I had ever prepared for, or imagined could happen in real life – car fires only happen in movies, right?

Movies. Car fires. Stuff exploding. What if my car is going to explode? What if I can't get my daughter out? Who do I call? What do I do? WHAT DO I DO?

My brain exploded with a million questions and possible scenarios. On the inside, I was melting. On the outside, I was calm and composed because I didn't want to frighten my daughter. I coolly put my hazard lights on, pulled the car over to the right shoulder, threw it in park, cut the engine, and popped open my door.

My heart was racing. I tried to calm my voice.

"Sweetie. We are going to get out of the car and walk down the road a bit. Everything is okay," I told my daughter. Though my body was moving fast, I tried to keep my voice low and slow. If my daughter saw I was calm, chances were she would remain calm too.

"Why, Daddy?" she asked as I fumbled with her car seat straps.

"The car is on fire, honey," I replied in a matter of fact tone. I was struggling with her car seat straps. I couldn't get her unlatched.

I COULDN'T GET HER UNLATCHED!

Movies. Car explosions. Gotta get her and run. How far? How far do I have to run? How much time do I have? HOW MUCH TIME DO I HAVE? WE HAVE TO RUN NOW!

I finally freed her from the stubborn straps. The man in the Jeep pulled over. He ran to my car and asked if there was anyone else inside. I said no and started to run from the car as fast as I could, clutching my daughter in my arms.

A truck pulled over and another man hopped out, grabbed a fire extinguisher seemingly out of nowhere, and put out the fire.

A fire that had been traveling down my fuel line.

The only fear my daughter had throughout the event was that her stuffed animal could have burned up with the car. My mother-in-law picked her up from the freeway and got her to school on time. The rest of her day was perfectly normal. Mine, however…

I waited on the freeway for my wife to pick me up. When she arrived, I sat in her passenger seat for a few moments. Silent.

I could have lost her. She could have been hurt. She could have –

The weight of the danger was replaced with the unbearable thought of what could have happened. And as I sat in the passenger seat, silently, the emotion engulfed me and the tears erupted. I cried, I sobbed, my shoulders that had recently been adorned with my daughter's arms, shuddered and rocked. I had never felt so powerless and fortunate in the same moment.

I would like to pretend I acted like an action hero – that I pulled the door off the hinges, ripped her from the car seat and dashed faster than the Flash down the freeway, away from the car. The truth is, the experience was humbling. I was trembling the whole time and know how close to disaster we came, which is why I still get a lump in my throat when I tell people: "My car caught on fire."

Creed Anthony *is a son, little brother, husband, father of two, Indy Dads Group organizer and teacher. He writes as "The Captain" at www.talesfromthepoopdeck.com. He is also a frequent contributor at LifeofDad.com and BalconyDads.com.*

REVENGE OF THE STOMACH FLU

John Engel, Florence, MA

It's Friday, 2:55 p.m., and my cell phone vibrates. When I see it is the director of Zoe's preschool calling, a pit forms in my stomach. In the past month, half the town has been sick with one malady or another. Just two weeks ago we weathered a respiratory virus that knocked out three family members. We considered ourselves fortunate since the bodily fluids involved only required a few boxes of tissues. This past weekend, we had all returned to 100 percent.

But this morning, by the time I returned from dropping off our high-spirited five-year-old Zoe at school, my wife, Lori, had hit the deck with gastro-intestinal symptoms, a burst of chills, dizziness and a fever.

So when I answer the call, it is no surprise to learn that our little Zoe had just tossed her lunch.

As I enter the building, I pass one of Zoe's teachers who, having just mopped up, is on his way to the dumpster. In the hallway outside her classroom sits two knotted trash bags: one containing her clothes, the other her naptime bedding. Inside, Zoe is pale and nursing a bucket. On our way out, Zoe leaves one more special deposit in the parking lot. At least we weren't in the car, I think to myself.

At home, after Zoe purges a few more times, and with no sign of a quick recovery for Lori, I snap into super-domestic-hero mode. "I will not get sick," is my mantra. I set the washing machine to heavy-duty and mix a cocktail of bleach, vinegar and soap for six consecutive jumbo loads of laundry. I spin from room to room like a madman, a bandana covering my face and rubber gloves up to my elbows, washing and sanitizing sinks, floors, beds and anything else that cannot be thrown in the trash, dishwasher or washing machine.

By dinner time, Adam our two-year-old, who has spent the afternoon running back and forth checking on his mama, still horizontal in our bed, and his big sister, stretched out on a camping pad in the living room, is the only one with an appetite. He is delighted to know that, since I have no energy for whipping up a wholesome meal, he is going to eat frozen waffles. He pumps both fists in the air and yells: "Yeah baby!"

On Saturday morning, Zoe and Lori still have the "run over by a truck" look. Making up for the rest of us, Adam knocks back six bowls of cereal and is starting to get a bit cagey. A trip to the transfer station, where he is beside himself with the presence of all things heavy-duty: snow-plows, dump trucks, diggers, etc., is the perfect outlet. By evening, Lori is starting to turn the corner and – despite hours of spooning with his sick mama and slugging drinks from his sick sister's water bottle – Adam shows no signs of illness. I decide my persistent queasiness is a figment of my imagination. Just to be sure, I adopt a no eat, no throw-up policy.

Sunday arrives and, with the girls clearly on the mend. Super-domestic-hero blood still coursing through my veins, I decide, like any sensible father would, to finish painting the master bathroom. This proves useful in three ways. One, I am able to check off a major item on the honey-do list. Two, I have ample time to obsess about the list of work deadlines that have started piling up while I have been operating a home-based urgent care clinic. Three, I can effectively distract myself from my increasing sense of malaise.

Before the paint dries, I go down, hard. Claiming the bed Lori has finally vacated, I wallow in misery all through the night. Time slows to a glacial pace. At first I tell myself, "I won't get sick." When my health does not improve, clinging to hope, I think, "Yeah, I might get sick, but maybe not." From the moment I accept the inevitability of my situation, until it actually happens, seems like an eternity.

Monday afternoon, feeling like I just might live, Zoe climbs up onto the bed and sits next to me. Just as I had done for her on Saturday, she sings to me "You Are My Sunshine," and then leans over and kisses my forehead. In that moment, I realize nothing feels as precious as a father's love for his sick little girl – except a little girl's love for her sick daddy.

***John Engel** is a father, husband, organizational consultant and writer. He is Director of The Fatherhood Journey, with a mission to promote private and public conversations about fatherhood. His monthly column, 'The Fatherhood Journey,' runs in the Daily Hampshire Gazette and is available at www.fatherhoodjourney.com. John is also Coordinator of the Healthy Men and Boys Network of Western Massachusetts, which can be viewed at www.hmbnetwork.org.*

HOW DO I TELL HIM?

Jason Grant, Riverdale, NY

"Argh, Aaargh, Mmmh."

"Daddy, what is that?" came the sweet, delicious voice of my now four-year-old son in the back seat of the car. It was the first time he verbally responded to my vocal tics.

"Oh … nothing," I lied.

Nothing? Is Tourette's syndrome nothing? Not to me, it isn't. The years of torment from schoolmates and perfect strangers who misunderstood my tics wasn't nothing. The years of having to make an announcement whenever my vocal tics appeared on the crowded subway or on a plane wasn't nothing.

"I'm sorry everyone, please don't mind that. I have Tourette's syndrome."

People seemed to be able to handle hearing a crying baby on board more easily than my monotonous vocalizations.

I should be used to it by now. I was diagnosed at the age of 11. Now I'm 42.

The memories never fade, though. Coping doesn't get easier.

"I'm going to have to tell junior about it, you know," I whispered to my wife in the driver's seat. "Do I tell him now?"

"Be rational," she said. "You're going to explain Tourette's to a four-year-old little boy?"

She was right. At least, it gave me some time to figure out how to explain it to him. If I did not say it the right way, I feared he would become apprehensive and nervous around me.

"F*ck!" I shouted. This I couldn't blame on the TS. My particular case does not give me the compulsion to shout obscenities. It was me, all me, being angry, being angry I had to explain why his daddy was different.

"Language," she chided me. "He hears you."

"When do I tell him?" I asked.

"You're getting yourself more nervous than you have to be. And now your tics will get worse. He'll be old enough to understand on a basic level in a couple of years," she replied. "But don't worry, he'll be fine with it."

Yeah. He'll be fine with it. Will he be fine with it on the Metro North when people switch seats to avoid having to sit next to us because of my tics? What is he going to think when the two of us are at the movies together and I bark or grunt and people sitting around us tell me to "shut up"? I don't want him to be ashamed or hesitant to be around me or to bring a girlfriend home when he's older … much, much older.

"Do you think he'll be too embarrassed to have his friends meet me?" I pressed her.

"You're over-thinking it, sweetheart, he'll love you. Nothing will change."

"How will I explain it to him though? I know I can't say, 'Daddy has a genetic neurological condition called Tourette's syndrome that causes him to make involuntary muscle twitches and vocalizations called tics.'"

"You've done it before, you'll do it again."

"When did I tell him?"

"Not our son, you goof. Carly. How did you explain it to her four years ago?"

Four years ago we took our goddaughter to brunch and a ball game in New York City. It was the first time I had to explain Tourette's to any child. She was six-years-old at the time and she unexpectedly asked why I made "those noises."

I remembered asking her nervously, "Well, can you stop yourself from sneezing?"

"No," she responded.

"Well, sometimes I make sounds or twitches and I can't stop it. Just like a sneeze."

"Oh," she said. "Does it hurt?"

"No. Not really," I re-assured her. "It's nothing to worry about."

"Are you enjoying your French toast and eggs with us right now?" my wife asked her.

"Yes."

"Are you looking forward to going with us to the baseball game later?"

"Yes."

"Does Jason seem different now that you know what we told you about him?"

"No. He's just the same old major league goofball he's always been."

"Well. You're right." I said proudly. "I'm not different. I'm still the same old goofball I've always been. You're still my friend, and I'm still yours."

Remembering my talk with Carly that day took a lot of weight off my shoulders.

"I feel better now," I said calmly. "I'll tell the little monkey the same way I told Carly and he'll still love me. The fact that I have Tourette's won't change our relationship a bit. He loves me and he knows I love him back."

Lori laughed, "That's what I've been trying to tell you! Jake will love you because you love him, because you take care of him every day and because you are his Daddy."

"As it should be."

***Jason Grant** is a full-time dad, a contributing blogger for the NYC Dads Group, and a professional writer who spreads awareness of Tourette syndrome and its related disorders. By far, the best and most challenging job Jason has ever held is being Jake's Daddy. You can read more about them at http://www.daddylogue.com/.*

PART FOUR

DO IT YOURSELF DADS

"My goal is to show them the parts of the world that will mean something to them, while warning them of the parts that will get in their way. All that is way more important than a tidy house."

- Jim O'Dowd, father of four from Boulder, CO

FIFTY SHADES OF PIG

Shannon Carpenter, Lee's Summit, MO

If you look closely, and perhaps from the side, it kind of looks like a pig. And by that, I mean it's pink and has what could be generously called ears. Kind of. The eyes are certainly off. One eye looks like it's growing out of the pig's head, the other is lopsided and by its nose. If you've ever seen the movie *Goonies* and the character Sloth, that's pretty much what I have drawn on this kid's face. But it's a pig, hand to God, it's a pig. Or it's supposed to be a pig.

I wasn't meant to do face painting. On so many levels, my very being is against it. I have big sausage fingers and I often scrape my Neanderthal knuckles by just making the bed. I am made for making big sweeping movements, wrapping arms around little individuals for big hugs or perhaps moving a piano down a flight of stairs. I am not good at detailed, minute movements. The dexterity required to paint a pig on a little girl's face requires control I really just don't have. If I was a brain surgeon, I would have killed everyone. But if you need a rock moved, I'm probably your guy.

Oh, and I have zero artistic talent. I would probably need that as well as finger dexterity.

I wasn't supposed to be doing any face painting. That wasn't in the cards when I signed up to volunteer at my kids' school carnival. No, I was to run the inflatable obstacle course. That was the deal. At my kids' school, that's what the dad volunteers do. I take a kid, throw him inside, and then hide his shoes when he's not looking. That's the job you want me for.

I had just finished my shift at the inflatable obstacle course. My kids were still having a good time spending their little game tickets so I sat down in the gym with one of the other dads I see twelve times a week because our kids do a lot of the same things. I like him. He's a cool dude. That's where I planned to spend the remainder of my evening. Then I would go home and have glass of wine with my sausage fingers. Perhaps some cheese. I'm fancy.

However, I was hijacked. The volunteer coordinator rushed up to us. "I need your help," she pleaded. What is it? Is someone stuck in a tree? Is there a rock that needs to be moved?! Yes, I will help. Let's go sidekick. Let's go help! I lack only a cape and a secret identity.

"Okay, you two sit here. There are the stencils and there is the face paint," she said after delivering us to the face painting station.

I thought it was a joke. Ha Ha, good one. Where is the air conditioning unit you want me to lift up?

Nope, not a joke. Apparently we were short of volunteers for this carnival. Something about an "ice storm coming." I don't know, I just go where I'm needed. Like Batman. Or a brain surgeon. So now I'm face painting.

The little girl ran up and wanted a pig, oh a pig would be so great! I did not have a stencil for a pig. I tried to convince her that perhaps a nice skull and cross bones would be better suited to our situation. Nope, she wanted a pig.

So I gave my best shot at a pig and when it was done it looked like a poor science experiment you want to put out of its misery and then stuff into a little formaldehyde jar.

"Now do a kitty cat on the other side!" she said.

Turns out that my kitty cat looks a lot like my pigs, only the kitty cat is somewhat orange and appears to have a mustache.

The next kid wanted a unicorn. I suggested a tank or perhaps an American flag? Nope, she wanted a unicorn. For those that don't know, a unicorn looks like a pig but it's white and it has a weird spear coming out of its forehead. I nailed that unicorn.

On and on this went. Different shades of pigs really. I assumed I would get better at this as time went on and I got more practice. Nope, my different arrays of pigs pretty much just changed shades.

"I want Batman," a little boy asked. Hell yes, I can give you some Batman! After a good ten minutes, I gave him Batman Pig. Close enough. I also did one mustache. You would think a bearded man could do this pretty well. Not so much. My mustache looked worse than a pig, like some poor soul suffering from leprosy.

My son came to my booth and wanted his face painted. He said he would let me choose because he didn't know what he wanted. I love my boy, I really do. So I gave my son horns. Or to the untrained observer, red pigs.

It's important to me that my kids see me involved with their school and activities. I know it sets a good example and it also shows them I am interested in what is going on in their lives. I don't want to be a casual observer, I want to be a part of them. Sometimes that means I coach a team or run an inflatable bounce house. And other times that means I paint the creatures from the Island of Dr. Moreau onto the faces of their classmates.

Shannon Carpenter *is a strapping older gentleman who enjoys the occasional donut topped with chocolate. And sprinkles, yeah sprinkles. Sprinkles are the bomb. As a stay-at-home dad for the last seven years, he vows to take all comers in the speed diaper changing challenge. With three kids who have pushed him to his limits, he has learned to love, to laugh and to make really good sour cream enchiladas. Read more of his adventures at http://thehossmanfamily.blogspot.com. Two of Shannon's stories also appeared in* Dads Behaving DADLY: 67 Truths, Tears and Triumphs of Modern Fatherhood.

LEAVES OF FOLLY

Richard Blake, Lafayette, CO

The neighbors think I'm crazy. There are a host of my quirky behaviors that could account for this opinion, but today's activity with my children surely confirms any suspicions they may already have. Corinne, my precocious three-year-old girl, Eliot, my exuberant five-year-old boy, and I, a middle-forties full time at-home dad, are knocking on our neighbors' doors asking them if we can rake their leaves.

"How much?" each neighbor asks.

"We don't need any money," our little triad says in unison.

"What do you want our leaves for?" they respond, as if we are vacuum salespeople offering a no-obligation free house cleaning but who fail to mention it comes with an excruciatingly long presentation on the benefits of their product.

Corinne begins to bounce up and down and shouts, "We want them to make a leaf pile!"

The Aspen trees that once encircled the small backyard in our slice of suburbia have been slowly dying over the last few years, leaving only an oak and spruce tree standing. What had been a glorious cache of falling leaves in previous falls had trickled to near nothing. Despite their young age, Eliot and Corinne already had indelible and fond memories of jumping into leaf piles during our yard's golden age. Ever since the swelter of summer switched abruptly to the chill of fall, Corinne and Eliot have been asking when we will have a leaf pile so they can play in it. I had been stalling for weeks with the simple and noncommittal, "I don't know." Now that the neighborhood yards are two or more inches deep in crispy, leafy gold, I can put them off no longer. Though I explained many times we don't have enough trees in our yard to generate the most basically serviceable leaf pile, the two of them have persisted in their questioning.

I realize the time has come to give a definitive answer, and there is only one possible answer: "How about today?"

"But where will we get the leaves?" asks Eliot. Apparently my assertions about the lack of leaves in our yard have finally hit home.

"Let's see if the neighbors will give us their leaves," I suggest.

Our first two stops at neighbors' houses yield no success. The third neighbor is much more amenable to our plan but does not want a leaf pile in the middle of her yard because of how it might harm her grass. She suggests we pile the leaves into the street and jump in them there. I am not sure why she thinks having two children leap, full force, into a pile of leaves sitting atop an unyielding piece of blacktop seems like a good idea. I instead offer to gather up all her leaves and take them to our yard.

She stares at me in silence, her mind churning out the implications of my suggestion. "You mean, you want to take the leaves from my yard and dump them into your own yard because you don't have enough leaves to rake up in your yard?"

"Yes," I reply confidently, aware of the lunacy in what I am proposing. I could feel the hope rising from behind me as Eliot and Corinne begin bobbing in place. I break out in sweat, trying to will the word "yes" into the neighbor's head. She continues, ". . . and then you'll have to rake them all back up yourself again later?" She is now speaking in the way villainous robots do in B sci-fi movies when they are about to say, "That does not compute!" before exploding.

"Okay," she slowly agrees, adding "But be careful of the grass." Glancing down at the brownish blades of her lawn that are occasionally visible through the leafy carpet, I promise we will.

I begin blowing the leaves toward the edge of the yard where Corinne and Eliot, suitably armored in heavy jackets, leather child-sized gloves, ear protection and comparatively miniature goggles, are eagerly waiting to collect our booty into oversized bags. In short order, my helpers realize an entirely adequate pile of leaves is forming right in front of them and begin jumping into it rather than scooping it up. I remind them the neighbor did not want us playing in her yard and they dutifully return to work.

During our labors, another neighbor emerges with a leaf blower and begins pushing the leaves from his yard out into the street. I take a quick break, asking him if we can have his leaves. He stares at me for a moment and then agrees.

And so the afternoon passes, the kids and I gathering up leaves into bags, hauling those bags into our backyard, dumping them, and returning to get more. Though the pile is now substantial, the lure of more and more leaves with the potential of building a mound that rivals the Tower of Babble keeps driving us from yard to yard. When the people who live on either side of our shared fence come home and begin raking their yards, we ask them if they would consider dumping their leaves over the fence to us. In both cases incredulous looks are followed by hesitant agreement and then enthusiastic compliance.

By the time my wife Becca gets home, we now have a pile of leaves as tall as our fence and about twelve feet wide on either side. "Oh boy!" she exclaims as her children run to greet her before dashing full force into the pile for the first time. Becca laughs at their joy and we stand there, admiring their exuberance as they burrow deep into the mound and disappear, save for their riotous laughter.

Before going in to change out of her work clothes, my wife turns to me and quietly says "You know you're gonna have to clean all this up, right?"

***Richard Blake**, a child since birth, provides full time care for two amazing kids and part time frustration for a wonderful wife at his centrally located Colorado home. Prior to his current role as master of his domestic domain, Richard held highly skilled but entirely unappreciated positions in academia and corporate America. Brain care specialist Gag Halfrunt had this addition to Mr. Blake's biography: „Vell, Richard's just zis guy, you know?"*

THE MAGIC MOOSE WAND

N.D. Richman, Calgary, AB, Canada

The crack was loud. It boomed through the trees, broke my thoughts, and stopped me in my tracks. I peered into the forest on my left but could see nothing under the dark canopy.

I turned back to Thomas. He looked as though he had just seen the world's largest ice cream cone.

I flashed back to the days leading to our first overnight stay, deep in the backcountry of Kananaskis, Alberta. I had packed the kids' backpacks, not with excitement but with trepidation. Thomas was only five, Michael six and Christopher nine. There are only a few people in the backcountry and no means to communicate with the outside world. What if one of them got sick or hurt? I had wondered. What if I got hurt and they were left alone to fend for themselves? Was I being stupid or selfish? I had pushed the worries away. "You can't keep them locked in a bubble," I had told myself.

As I stared into Thomas's eyes, seeing his excitement and fear, the worries flooded back. Having hiked around Upper Kananaskis Lake and into the valley on the other side, we hadn't seen a soul and were four miles into the trip. A river raged to our right and the forest on our left rose to a granite peak, somewhat obscured by the trees surrounding us. If an animal cornered us, there was no way of escape.

Thomas looked back into the forest and his mouth dropped. Michael and Christopher stepped up beside him and peered into the trees.

"It's a moose, Dad," Christopher whispered.

My stomach sunk. Moose stand up to seven feet tall at the shoulder, weigh up to 1,500 pounds, and can be extremely unpredictable. I had hoped the kids were wrong. "Don't move," I whispered back.

I crept back to my children and peered into darkness. The moose stood out as easily as if she was standing in line at a McDonald's. She was twelve feet away and looking straight at us.

Fears tore through my mind. What if she charges? What does she want? Is she alone? How do I protect my children?

I told the kids not to make any sudden moves and bunched them in front of me. Tightly pressed together, we stumbled down the trail. I prayed the moose would stay and this would soon be over.

The moose did not stay. She kept abreast of us for forty feet. We stopped and the moose stopped. We walked and the moose walked the exact same pace.

We continued but the moose was determined. She was not going to go away.

I decided to wait the moose out. I guided my children into the hollow of a fallen tree, turned to the moose and stared her down. She stared back.

I can't tell you how long this standoff lasted, but at some point the moose moved forward. I breathed a sigh of relief as she continued ahead, but my relief grew to horror when she stopped twelve feet down, walked to the trail and turned, facing me directly. We were pinned between the forest and the river. The trail was three feet wide and a moose, towering two feet above me, blocked our path.

I literally forgot to breath. I looked down at my children. They peered over the tree trunk at the moose. They seemed excited, not understanding the danger. If the moose were to take me down, they'd be left in the back country with no one to protect them, with no way to get home, with no father.

Three minutes had gone by. The moose hadn't budged. I was desperate. It was then I realized I was holding a rolled up mattress pad in my hand. I had removed it off of Thomas's backpack earlier to reduce the weight of his pack. It was useless against a moose but I did the only thing I could with it. I pointed it at the moose like the sword Excalibur and said in a commanding voice, "Go!"

To this day, I could swear I saw the moose shrug. It charged two steps towards me, swung left, and crashed down the embankment and splashed into the river, crossing it and vanishing into the forest on the other side.

I breathed. The children laughed.

"Hey, Dad," Christopher said, "that's a magic moose wand."

To this day a rolled up mattress pad is called a magic moose wand in our family.

This adventurous trip to the backcountry preceded five more trips, one per year. I've never regretted taking my children, for the adventures we had together were life experiences, never to be forgotten.

N.D. Richman *is a self-employed automation technologist and is currently working as an engineering manager. He has been married to his high school sweetheart, Tracy, for 28 years and is the father of four teenage children: Christopher, 20, Michael, 17, Thomas, 16, and Katherine, 14. As a graduate of the Outward Bounds wilderness survival school, he loves hiking and camping in the Canadian Rockies. In order to interest his reluctant reader, Michael, he has written the* Boulton Quest Series *of books a favorite of preteens throughout the world. Find him at www.ndrichman.com.*

PRINCESS DRAFT

Art Eddy III, Stanhope, NJ

The NFL Draft has become a huge spectacle for fans to watch. There are some who think it is a complete waste of time to watch three days of giant men in suits shaking hands with the NFL Commissioner. It's not like a game is going on!

For me, I beg to differ. Not only have I enjoyed watching the draft, but it inspired a solution for my arguing toddlers not unlike what I imagine was the reason for the very first NFL Draft. This might sound crazy, but dealing with two kids fighting over plastic dolls brings along its own zaniness.

One evening while I was making dinner, I heard my four-year-old and two-year-old daughters fighting over who gets Cinderella and who gets Ariel. I thought to myself, "here we go again." One wants what one can't have. I was a bit frustrated they were fighting over two dolls, but they are kids. Siblings fight, so why should my daughters be any different?

As the fight ensued and became louder, I knew I had to intervene, primarily for my own sanity. Dealing with toddlers by using adult logic, however, does not work. So I thought, why not have a Princess Draft?

It works for the NFL, so maybe it could work here.

I put the entire princess lineup on the coffee table surrounded by the seven dwarfs and princes to act like their family and friends, just like the college players have at the NFL Draft. That attention to detail went unnoticed by my girls. I was a little hurt, but I moved on. I had dinner cooking in the other room so I didn't have time to sweat the small stuff.

To see who picked first I put a crayon in one of my hands and asked my youngest, Jordan, to pick which hand the crayon was in. I explained if Jordan guessed correctly she would pick first and if she didn't, Lily would pick first. As I saw them glaze over me and look at the princesses, I knew

I had to keep the draft moving or there would be a renewal of hostilities. Plus, was something burning in the kitchen?

Jordan guessed the wrong hand, so Lily went first. Following the likes of draft experts Mel Kiper and Todd McShay, the Princess Draft experts Flora, Fauna, and Merryweather predicted correctly that Cinderella would be the overall first pick selected by Lily. Belle was a surprise pick at number two by Jordan while we saw Lily pick Rapunzel at the third spot. Lily then pulled a real draft day deal asking to have Ariel and Snow White if Jordan would take the rest. This consisted of Sleeping Beauty, Jasmine, Mulan, and Tiana. Jordan, at first, did not like the fact that she would skip her turn, but when I told her she would have more dolls than Lily, she made the deal.

I was proud of the trade. It showed me that my daughters got the idea of sharing and taking turns. It was what I hoped they would learn through the Princess Draft. Fans get it through the NFL Draft. Well, except for Jets fans, maybe. I know kids, especially at their age, will start fights about things that seem ridiculous to parents, but we were kids once. We need to remember what is important to them. Getting a chance to play with a certain doll ranks really high in their world. In our house we use the phrase "sharing is caring." Sure, it's a bit of a cliché, but my wife and I want to instill compassion in our kids.

I was really excited to see my draft idea worked for both them and me. They went back to playing nicely with each other and I got to focus on not burning dinner.

As parents, we don't want to see our children fighting with each other, but it will happen. What we want to do is have them learn from those disagreements. We want to show them there is always an opportunity for a solution no matter the stakes. I felt I was able to teach them that if you do things in a manner both parties feel is fair, you can easily come to an understanding.

I felt like the Princess Draft was an enormous success! Next year I hope to have the draft televised live on ESPN 8 The OCHO! I figure, Disney owns ESPN so it's possible, right?

Art Eddy III *is an at-home dad. He and his wife Jess are blessed with two daughters, Lily and Jordan. Art is a writer for www.LifeOfDad.com and produces two podcasts on that site:* The Life of Dad Show *and* The Life of Dad After Show. *Art loves making his family laugh, doing crafts with his daughters, and just hanging out with his family. A self-proclaimed sneakerhead, Art also loves anything that deals with Star Wars, 49ers, Bulls and Red Sox.*

A HILL OF BEANS

Ryan A. Bell, Berkeley, CA

"Mom, give the baby some of your beans." I said.

"Beans?" my mother replied as though it were some unfamiliar word.

"Yes, Poppy loves beans."

"She eats beans?" my mother replied, again with eyes as vacant as a Detroit Nordstrom.

My mother and her boyfriend, Randall, were visiting for our Thanksgiving gathering that was just two short days away. They average one visit every six months and have a difficult time keeping their eyes off the baby.

Poppy, at the head of the table, was stretching the straps of her booster seat to its very limits, reaching for the delicious and protein-filled black beans on my mother's plate. I loved giving her beans and welcomed the healthy dark poops the next day. They were the base that countered the acids Poppy craved and kept her diaper rash at bay. They were fun, time-consuming and taught her fine motor skills. I loved giving my daughter beans so much I didn't even mind the farts that would slowly be filtering out of her diapers tomorrow.

"Yes," I repeated, "Poppy loves beans."

My wife shot me a quick look from the kitchen sink. I couldn't tell if it was consternation, warning or commiseration. My sister-in-law, Michelle, squirmed in her seat a little but said nothing.

"She'll eat beans, huh?" mother said with her head cocked Golden Retriever style still looking at the child.

"Yes," I said losing only a little bit of cool, "Beans are seriously her favorite."

My mother looked up at the light above the dining room table to take in all of this new information.

"You," I continued, "should give her some of the ones that you have…"

"They might be hot …" she said opening up another window in this conversations browser.

"Spicy hot or temperature hot?" I asked, all the while knowing they were neither.

"I don't know really …" She studied the beans again. She had turned the fork upside down and was using it to point at the beans. "Maybe both since she's a baby."

"You do know that she eats pretty much everything and she loves beans, right?"

"Well, do you think that she'll like these beans?" my mother asked.

My sister-in-law couldn't take it anymore. The squirming had turned into a visible chin jutting and exhalation exercise.

"Give her," an uncharacteristically low voice came from Michelle, "some beans."

My mother rotated the fork over as slowly as one would push a very large roll of carpet up a hill, until the four-pronged utensil was in the appropriate position. All eyes were on the tendons working inside of her long and graceful fingers manipulating it. Poppy's mouth was agape in anticipation for a helping of deliciously dark black beans that dripped in black bean juice and promised wonderfully funny tomorrow farts.

The fork touched down upon the beans and methodically separated a solitary bean from the group and proceeded to bring the lonely bean onto Poppy's plate. My child looked down at the bean and then up at her grandmother with obvious concern. I imagined she worried she would starve to death at this rate of feeding.

"There you go Pop!" my mother said with pride.

"Come on mom," I was losing the facade of patience. "I didn't say give her a single bean. I asked for you to give her some of your beans."

My wife's eyes were widening in the kitchen. It was becoming more and more apparent that something was going to go down. Were we at the cusp of The Great Bean War of 2014? Was this going to be the holiday fight that ended in tears and the painful I'm-sorry-hugs I didn't mean?

It was the heartbreaking way my world often worked with my mother. She would methodically push me to my limit and break me down. Then we would fight and she would have the opportunity to be hurt. I would apologize for being angry, while despising her for getting me there.

I've learned a few things as a dad, so I decided to change up our usual script.

"Here," I said to my mother, "let me help."

I took my own fork, grabbed a sloppy pyramid of beans and dropped them on Poppy's plate. My daughter's eyes widened again as she picked up her own fork, shoveling the beans into her mouth as best she could.

"May I?" I asked my mother.

"Of course!" she said, excited to be included.

I grabbed another forkful of beans and put them on her plate. My mother's eyes locked on her granddaughter. I could visibly see how much she loved that child. She craned in closer to Poppy and her eyes glistened. I thought about the way she was looking at her and the way that my mother hadn't taken her eyes off of the baby.

I'd been completely wrong. My mother wasn't looking for a fight. The focus she had on this child made every single thing in the world a whisper. Her eyes had been "glistening" this entire trip because she was always so very close to crying out of sheer joy.

Now, finally, as a parent, I know that just-about-to-bust feeling you have when you love something so much you are just unable to contain it. It's a feeling that if you were to cut open your chest, you wouldn't be surprised if the world quickly became covered in confetti and candy and Pachelbel's Canon in D playing so loudly the ground shook. The seams of my mother were barely holding these emotions in.

As a dad who is often too busy or hung up in his own BS, I seem to forget that my own parents have felt this way and still feel this way about me. I also forget they don't have as much time with my child as I do or, for that matter, as much time as I have left on this earth.

My family is more sacred than difficult. I plan to do a better job not sweating the small stuff even when there's a whole bunch of it.

After all, being pissed off doesn't really amount to a hill of beans anyhow.

***Ryan A. Bell** is proud to be the only man ever referred to as "World's Hairiest Mom Blogger" AND "Southern Fried Feminist." As a native Georgian living in Berkeley, he's a mix of advocate, comedian, poet, blogger, MC, evangelist and critic. Always outspoken and often rough around the edges, Ryan tackles tough subjects with humor, love and enough tact to not offend (most of the time). He's an active advocate for breastfeeding, LGBT rights, HIV awareness, anti-bullying and he volunteers so much with Special Olympics and youth organizations that he recently won The Presidential Award for Volunteer Service and recognized by CBS' People of Distinction. Follow his shenanigans on at www.daddyissues123.com, www.iamnotthebabysitter.com and on Twitter and Facebook.*

BONDING ON BROADWAY

Vincent Fitzgerald MSW LSW, Jersey City, NJ

Fag. Queer. Mary. Those incendiary words were often fired off during verbal wars waged in my adolescence to assassinate character. Emasculation was the mortal wound inflicted upon misunderstood Omega males too shy to talk to girls or who failed to excel on the fields of play. I was among the guilty who discharged the rounds, apathetic toward the piercing hate and hurt, marginalizing a population about whom I knew nothing about.

The microcosmic world of college provided more than academics. The social education bore friendships with gay students with whom I shared my love of writing and reading, but with whom at one time I may have been afraid to share a men's room. Our time spent discussing authors, styles of writing, and politics scraped away stereotypes and revealed people. As a junior, I met David Blackmore, a progressive, gay professor whose passion for introducing students to ethnic writers ignited my desire to embrace authors of various cultures. I was drawn to him, admiring his obliteration of literary boundaries. Taking his classes made me all the more eager to work with him on my senior honors thesis. No teacher more profoundly impacted my formal and social education. When I met him, he was Professor Blackmore, but by graduation he was mentor, friend, and David, sculptor of the appreciation for diversity I hoped to one day relay to my own children.

When Emily was nine-years-old, I divorced her mother who became custodial parent. As Emily developed a relationship with her step-dad, I felt reduced to tertiary caregiver, struggling to elbow my way into her life. Though I was always unsure of my abilities as a father, returning her like a DVD rental was painful.

I am a passionate fan of Broadway's *Rent*, enthralled by its music and its message. The soundtrack plays on a loop in my car, and Emily absorbed it from the first time she heard its notes. When I first heard her sing "Seasons of Love" in her feathery voice, I swelled with pride over her tuned interest and the opportunity for a possible unique bond between just us. With her tenth birthday approaching, I decided to give Emily a controversial gift, but one I was sure would allow ample opportunity for teachable moments.

Wanting Emily to experience the spectacle and choreography of *Rent*, I purchased second row seats putting us within spitting distance of the straight, homosexual, and AIDS stricken characters. Emily was naive to the labels and the disease, prompting family and friends to question my judgment about sullying her innocence. *Rent* is not overtly sexual, and I believed I could explain to her anything she did not understand. The topics of AIDS and homosexuality made my inner circle queasy, but I had long since penetrated the show's surface, immersing myself in themes of love, the value of each minute, and the importance of community. I was certain of the opportunity to bond while teaching her the importance of understanding, tolerance, and acceptance would paint an indelible memory. Also, the stereotypes of homosexuality to which I had once subscribed to were a disease from which I wished to inoculate Emily.

I hyped the gift, telling Emily she could not touch it, but it would touch her. Our tickets were for a Saturday matinee during one of our weekends together. I asked her to pack a pretty outfit, further piquing her curiosity. From the moment I picked her up Friday night, Emily peppered me with questions to which I gave vague answers to spike her anticipation. The playfulness of the impromptu game of twenty questions warmed me, and Emily's frenzied excitement filled in the cracks formed by days of absence.

As we headed to New York City for the 2 p.m. matinee, Emily remained clueless to our destination. She looked elegant in her black dress, white heart embroidered over her own, and an ivory sweater draped over her shoulders. In my rearview mirror, I watched her eyes scan the city, marveling at the grandeur, the lights, and the rows of people walking in lockstep. Only when we turned on West 41st Street did Emily catch on. The blue of her widened eyes lit our car when she spotted the word *RENT* stenciled in black on a flashing white marquee. It was her birthday, but she gifted me with her smile.

From the opening note, I studied Emily's variety of facial expressions and her lips syncing the songs she had grown to love. I wondered what she was thinking as she watched male and female couples sing together with affection or hostility, constant references to a deadly disease mixed in.

During the car ride home, before popping in the soundtrack we had just heard performed live, Emily broke silence and barriers.

"Daddy, what's AIDS"?

Because my family was its own serious issue, other serious issues were never discussed as I grew up, making Emily's question a valued opportunity to bond through a teachable moment.

"It's a disease, Emmy. People get it in lots of ways: needles, blood transfusions, and sex." Venturing into tabooed terrain nauseated me a bit, but Emily knew how babies were made, saving me from further explanation on that one, so we talked about the disease that killed Angel, a central character, and the heart of the play. The discussion of Angel's death provided an easy segue to another difficult question.

"What's a lesbian?" her ethereal voice asked. The answer to her challenging question could possibly have shaped her opinions about sexual orientation for the rest of her life. This gave me an opportunity to lay the groundwork for a lifetime of appreciation of human diversity.

"A lesbian," I explained, "is a woman who is in love with another woman. There are different kinds of couples besides men and women, but they love each other the same way."

Having spent some years growing up in urban Jersey City, Emily had made friends with people of diverse cultures, but homosexuality and AIDS were more abstract concepts, not indicated by skin color or accent, and were far more stigmatized. I needed to be sure Emily did not grow up with the toxic thought processes by which I was once tainted. When I brought her home the next day, I no longer felt as though I rented my daughter. The experience assured me she was mine, and you are *What You Own.*

Exposing Emily to the musical I hoped would eradicate ignorance that had once been forced on me, was my primary goal, but not disclosing my secondary goal would be dishonest. I wanted something just for us; something remembered through songs, pictures, and the landscape of New York City. *Rent* provided that cherished Daddy/Daughter moment, along with a chance to shape her a bit. Emily trusted me when asking those imposing questions and the open dialogue assured me that taking her to the show was an appropriate decision. She learned about difficult social issues from me. Now in her senior year of high school, Emily possesses a social conscience I did not have at her age.

As a non-custodial father, I had to make the most of my opportunities to bond with my daughter and to teach her lessons I thought priceless. I am forever grateful to *Rent's* composer, Jonathan Larson, for birthing a piece of art I can share with Emily, one that opened a broad way of communication down which we continue to stroll together.

Vincent Fitzgerald MSW LSW, *born and raised in Jersey City, is currently a psychotherapist for the Nutley Family Service Bureau. He works with individuals, couples, and families, hoping to keep them intact during times of struggle. He has a 17-year-old daughter, Emily, and 12-year-old son, Aedan. As a divorced dad, he tries his best to do a better job than his father, remaining active in the lives of his kids.*

NIGHT NIGHT MOON

Matthew Brennan, Sugar Grove, IL

Our 21-month-old son Jamie only recently developed into a more cuddly stage. He has always been adorable, but that is tempered with his split second attention span. Until now, when I picked him up to sit him on my lap, he immediately scanned the room for his exit route, or next great adventure.

His mother and I have pounced on his newfound ability to sit for longer periods of time by establishing a nighttime reading ritual. Typically, we both put him to bed but it has been my job to read to him. It has been a great time for Jamie and I to bond while he sits in my lap to listen.

We read to him earlier, but it typically ended with him squirming out of our arms or strongly voicing his displeasure before the book was completed. Toddlers often have too much energy to sit still for any length of time. However, I believe it is an important skill I want to encourage and I hope my reading to him will create an interest in him to be an avid reader like me.

For the first year-and-a-half of Jamie's life, his mother and I worked different hours, giving me the opportunity to be highly involved in his daily routine. This offered me opportunities to bond with him during dinner or bath time and try to read to him when he wanted to listen. It gave me the opportunity to learn his personality and how he reacted in all different types of situations.

I love being involved and getting to know my son. Most toddlers jump and squirm from your lap as you try to pick them up, and my son was no different. The ability to sit still long enough for a full children's book is something he needed to ease into, and that began with paying attention to certain movie scenes.

At first he would sit for five or ten minutes, curious about what played on the television. Then he sat for longer. It quickly became clear he was picking things up while watching children's movies.

One evening my wife tried to pry a toy out of his hands.

"Let it go, Jamie," she told him.

"Let it go. Let it go. Elsa?" he replied.

He was probably a little over a year old when that exchange took place and we knew we had someone trying to piece things together. His attention span for movies increased. With that came his ability to sit still and occasionally watch from our lap. When that occurred, we knew it was our opportunity.

We had our chance to take advantage of his expanding attention span. The book we decided on was Good Night Moon by Margaret Wise Brown. It has become a regular part of our evenings. We will pick another book shortly to expand his horizons, but this one has seemed to foster a strong curiosity in him.

As I dress my son for bed each night, he is on his changing pad typically saying "Bye bye moon!" which is his way of asking me to read it to him.

I enjoy watching him put the various parts of the story together. Now, he can look at the pictures, finishing many of the sentences in the book. I point and he names the various objects. I have really come to enjoy working this brief but regular fixture into his nighttime routine.

The illustrations are so detailed in the book that Jamie began picking up other words that were not mentioned, such as fire, door and ball.

We have regularly read Jamie other books, but this is the quickest he has made an effort to put the words and story together. This is the first book he has learned to recognize on his own. He already began learning movies by the characters he likes—Elsa (Frozen), Buzz (Toy Story) and Mike Wazowski (Monster's Inc.).

Good Night Moon has prompted other nighttime rituals as he readies for bed. For instance, after we read the book, he now wants to look around the room, saying "night night" to his stuffed animals, blankets and other toys in the room. He even surprises us with words we did not know he knew.

The book sparked some interesting literary critiques between his mother and I as well. We questioned the logic between leaving a comb and a brush and a bowl full of mush on the nightstand. Perhaps that is what led to the mouse and, apparently, this family is okay with that. Also, it seems as though the illustrator missed a page since they say good night to nobody.

As soon as Jamie tires of Good Night Moon, he has a bookshelf full of options to continue reading.

***Matthew Brennan** is an Illinois writer documenting his experiences as a new dad. He has been published in Boys' Life, the Chicago Sun-Times, the Good Men Project and other various blogs, newspapers and magazines. He mainly writes about being a dad at his blog www.SpiralingUpwards.com.*

TICKLED PINK

Mike Sager, Lee's Summit, MO

There is a period of time when your kid starts to say words. At first it is only a few words, then there is that moment when they know there are more words, but frustration sets in as their will to say more is stifled by their limited vocabulary. Your ability to interpret what a two-year-old is saying is often influenced by how much time you have spent working on their words.

My daughter Claire went through a stage where she decided to stop using words. "Ummm," "ughhh," "ahhh ahhh ahhh," and a finger pointing at something was all I got. I saw other parents go through this. Many would tell their toddler to "use your words" or "tell me what you want." It has always been obvious to me this is not the issue at all. The kid knows how to say it, he or she just doesn't want to say it. This is a battle of wills. You either give in or beat your head against the wall while you kid teases you with guttural noises.

When Claire started doing this I would say, "Oh, you want to be tickled?" then I started tickling her frantically. No matter what the unintelligible word was, to me, it meant "Tickle me!" She would be forced to either resign to the fact that she was going to be tickled incessantly or would say, "NO, NO, I meant give me that!" Worked like a charm. Well, except when she gave an occasional gratuitous grunt for the express purpose of getting a little tickling. As a general rule, it worked and it worked far better than the head to head confrontations I saw other parents experience.

It seemed to me this method not only got her to use her words more often, but also built a desire in her to build on her vocabulary. Knowing what something was called was far safer than taking a risk that an off-hand "UHH" and a point would lead to a tickling session.

I found as time went on and her vocabulary expanded, the tickling incentive had other uses, beyond just getting her to use words.

One morning Claire was sitting on my lap before school. I was waiting for the time to leave and we were going over colors.

"How do you make green?" I asked.

"Blue and yellow!" she exclaimed.

"Very good. Now how do you make aquamarine?"

"I don't know," she offered.

"What do you mean you don't know? Of course you know what colors go together to make aquamarine."

"Give me a hint?" she said.

"Okay what color do you add to green to get aquamarine."

"Yellow?"

"No that's not it," I said as I tickled her and she giggled uncontrollably.

"Red?"

"No, that's not it," I said again, tickling her as she giggled.

"Orange?"

"No, you know what color it takes. What is it?" I did not tickle her this time. I felt it was time to actually verify she knew the right color.

She did not answer, instead demanding, "DAD you are supposed to tickle me!"

And there was her game. I started tickling her, "What color do you add to green to make aquamarine?" She was giggling uncontrollably. I tickled more, "What color do you add to green to make aquamarine?" She was still giggling and moving into that territory where it was almost too much laughter. "Stop, Dad stop." She pleaded. "Tell me what color!" I said. She was not giving up yet, "just stop dad stop!" her laughter had now moved into a running laugh, squeal she could not control, every part of her body was a trigger to bring more laughter.

"BLUE," she shouted, "BLUE AND GREEN MAKE AQUAMA-RINE!"

I stopped tickling her. As she sat beside me, squeezed into the office chair, I asked her, "What does green and yellow make?"

She giggled a bit, either left over from the previous assault or anticipation for the next one. I dangled my hand menacingly in front of her. She giggled uncontrollably, holding her hands in front of her guardedly. "Chartreuse!" she shouted. "Green and yellow make chartreuse!"

The rest of the color wheel proceeded without incident.

Mike Sager *is a stay-at-home dad to a daughter and a new baby boy. He has an MBA, is an active Civil War re-enactor, Girl Scout leader, storyteller, game designer, former CEO, and a damn fine cook. He sits on the board of directors of several charities and is known to put on beer, whiskey and wine tastings to raise money for his favorite causes. Mike and his family live in Missouri. Two of his stories also appeared in Dads Behaving DADLY: 67 Truths, Tears and Triumphs of Modern Fatherhood.*

OVER UNDER GAME

James Chapa, Downers Grove, IL

Our families are from the East Coast but, despite having lived in the Midwest for twenty-five years, we try to get together at the beach as often as possible. My kids have fond memories of swimming in the ocean from a very early age: racing in and out of the waves, boogie boarding, body surfing, and learning how to "read" the ocean.

When my kids were little one of the games we used to play was called "Over Under." The rules were quite simple. If a wave was green, you would ride over the top of it because you had time. If it was white and frothy, you would dive under it, and let it crash on the shore behind you. We would wade out into the water and everybody would be shouting "OVER!" or "UNDER!" and act accordingly. It was a great way to have fun in the waves while learning the power of the ocean. The accidental, occasional roll in the surf was a strong reminder to respect the ocean.

Late in the week of one of our vacations, as our families gathered on the beach for one more day in the sun, my impatient seven-year-old daughter wanted to play Over Under by herself. I said "sure." After all, she had a personal lifeguard watching her every move: me. The waves were pretty big that day, but she was an excellent swimmer, and I wasn't overly concerned. As she dashed out into the water, I rocked back into my chair, making small talk with family, occasionally glancing at my son digging his way to China like he did every day at the beach. Mostly, though, I was focused on my fish in the water.

I watched her judge the waves, jumping and playing in the water. Then, as an unusually large set of waves approached the shore, I watched to see how she would react. She did exactly as she should have, ducking under the first white wave and bobbing over the next two green ones. Now, however, she was a fair distance away from shore and treading water. The game had changed. I climbed out of my chair and walked down to the edge of the water, completely locked in on my little girl.

I could tell she knew she was, literally, in over her head. With big waves in front of her and big waves behind her, she couldn't see land from where she was. At this point, somebody who didn't know my girl as well as I did might have raced in to save her, but I wanted to see how she would react. I watched as she gauged wave after wave, working her way back to shore. I could tell she was scared. I thought my heart would explode out of my chest with pride and relief as she made it back into the "safe zone" where she could work her way back to the shore.

It was at about that time (which, I'll admit, seemed like an eternity), the rest of the family saw what was happening. My brother-in-law raced past me to "rescue" her, scooped her up, and placed her in my arms. "Thanks."

I'm not sure who was clinging to whom harder, but my little girl and I were both shaking with relief as I carried her back to the chairs. It was a scary moment for the both of us, but, as we like to paraphrase the Grinch around here, "her self-confidence grew three sizes that day."

***James Chapa** has been a stay-at-home dad for over 20 years to two children. While he's not ready to claim victory just yet, the early results are looking good. A serial home renovator, he liked to call himself an "On Home Dad" during the early years. James lives with his family in the Chicago area. One of his stories also appeared in Dads Behaving DADLY: 67 Truths, Tears and Triumphs of Modern Fatherhood.*

BORN TO RUN

Whit Honea, Oak Park, CA

We can run from dangers and to flights of fancy. We can run like a river between the canyons built tall around us. We can run away, and strong upon our course.

The younger one had always fallen to sport whenever the opportunity presented itself, which was far too seldom for his liking, dependent as it was upon my wallet and small hours salvaged from long, busy days.

The older did not care for games that demanded hits and throws or the trappings of competition. He had no desire to test his merit against the might of others. He preferred actions of the mind, sprawled across screens like so many battlefields. The only score he cared to best was the one he had set before it.

That is not to say that the latter did not take the time to kick a ball on occasion, and there were moments where he himself could understand the enjoyment in others, but as a rule the games did nothing for him.

Also true was that the former did develop a taste for the couch and the glossy-eyed dance between brain and thumb. He grew content there, in the shelter of his brother, and many days they would play until my wife or I bid them not to. It became clear the two boys would happily wile away their lives controlling puppets in the living room, the digital following of quick-handed orders, until the only memories they carried were red eyes and calluses.

And so we took to running.

It started over a year ago, when the older boy brought home demons in need of exorcise and I in need of a homophone. So we ran around the block, through streets and parks, up hills and down again, until all that was left were clear heads and hands on our hips.

We continued this whenever either of us was in the need with a pace set by conversation and the strength of his legs slowly matching the steel of his will. It soon became evident he had found his stride just as it was clearer still that I began to lose mine. He grew stronger, faster, and I grew weaker and more frail.

When the opportunity arose for him to join a club at school he took it. All I could do was drive him there to run laps around the campus while I sat at the stoplight on the corner, willing it to change.

It was the first time he had ever wanted to join anything on his own, not knowing a single student on the squad, and never bothering to take the time to learn the names of most of them. He was there to run, so that is what he did.

His younger brother found it akin to inspiration and wished to run a race as well. My wife, no stranger to long runs, agreed this was a thing to do together — a perfect team of individuals bound by blood and entrance fees.

It used to be that the skip in my stride was measured only by the pound of heartbeats and the growth of shadows flying straight from the sun. Then my legs lost their lean. I found myself hitting walls and leaving marks upon them like a well-fed Kilroy, brick by brick, and I felt them all come morning.

Those were the years where weight no longer waited, and my silhouette grew to block more from the scene, and all you could do was dare to peer around me.

When the boys were born, it became suddenly obvious, as important things tend to do, that I had let myself go, inch by inch — my breaths grew labored, my steps less fleet, and the only thing heavier than my excuses were the folds of my lap that turned to soft hills.

The kids were active and I had talked the talk as I walked beside them, encouraging them to take another lap while I stood in the grass and thought about it. The yard grew thick around my ankles, like a tree and throwing shade as I rooted.

And so we took to running.

It did not come easy. My body did what it could, and I crossed the finish line well behind my family, although none of us crossed together. The youngest ran three miles without ever looking back, and the oldest, not even twelve hours past a previous race through dirt-piled hills, finished somewhere behind him, torn, as he was, between nursing my pangs and finding his brother. My wife kept steady and provided words of encouragement every time she passed me.

We were tired legs and laughter.

There is no need to be lost in order to find yourself amid a throng of strangers, to trim the ivy from the walls we are afraid to hit. It is as if they are able to see what you cannot, the will that we bury between the rocks of homework and the hard place of deadlines — it connects us — and in each of us is the way of the other. We are all different and we are all the same; we are running and it moves us.

Then there is the finish line, and it feels so much more like starting.

***Whit Honea** is the author of* The Parents' Phrase Book *and co-founder of Dads4Change.com. His writing can be found all over the Internet including his personal site at whithonea.com. He lives in Los Angeles with his wonderful wife, two great boys, and way too many pets.*

ALL WET (THE 501 POOLSIDE BLUES)

Pete Wilgoren, South Pasadena, CA

We were running behind like always. One birthday party down and one to go. The kids and I rushed home so they could put on their bathing suits and grab their goggles for a pool party to celebrate a nine-year-old's birthday. I pictured a little backyard pool, but I was going to stay with them because I don't trust the "drop off" parties or pools I haven't seen before. I just don't.

We arrived and discovered it wasn't a backyard pool. It wasn't a backyard at all. It was an Olympic-sized pool at a community park, the type with platforms on the end and lanes to race in. I was glad I was there. My eight-year-old is an excellent swimmer and can race across the pool in deep water. My five-year-old, however, was still learning. She was great in the shallow end but loved to goof off and could not be trusted in the pool by herself.

Despite all the rushing around, I was sure I had thought of everything. This dad was cooking on all cylinders! Standing there with two girls in their bathing suits, something was nagging at me, though. I wondered what I had missed. I put my hand in my jeans pocket while I pondered. What had I missed? God I love these jeans, so comfortable. Hmmm. Holy crap! I forgot my swimsuit! I am at the pool with two kids for a pool party wearing a pair of jeans. Holy crap! Damn! Damn! Damn! Damn! I was so busy getting the girls ready and out the door I forgot about me. Crap!

My eight-year-old swam off like a fish. My five-year-old had the puppy dog eyes because she was sad and ready to jump in too. I thought for a moment. I looked at the other party parents. I thought some more. I looked at my five-year-old. I sucked up any little sliver of self- respect I had and I went for it. I went right into the pool with jeans, belt and all.

There I was in my jeans and my five-year-old swimming around, happy as a clam. Some of the partygoers winced. The pool staff laughed and shrugged. But there we were. For the next two hours I chased the five year old around the pool during the party in jeans.

When we got out of the pool, people gawked again. Jeans stick to the skin I learned. Jeans weigh you down like a denim albatross. I did the walk of shame while I got towels for the girls. I didn't think to bring a towel for myself either. We stood there and sang happy birthday to the birthday girl while a large puddle of water formed at my jean cuffs. Slowly I could feel a weight lifting from me as the jeans wrung themselves out. We said our goodbyes. The birthday girl's mom thanked us for coming and then proceeded to tell me that I was the highlight of the party. Her husband is a comedian by trade and I told her I was worried I would be hearing about myself in a future routine. I grabbed the girls and we sloshed right on out of there, leaving a set of wet tracks behind us.

Leather seats in cars love wet jeans. I put down towels and old clothes on the seat and sat right inside. It was all in a day's work for this dad. It made me realize we do so much for our kids. Sometimes we need to make sure we're not forgetting something. Until then, just call me Denim Dad or the Dungaree Dad, or the dad who showed up at the pool party and found a unique way to overcome the 501 blues.

Pete Wilgoren *is Managing Editor at one of the largest local news stations in the United States. He has won several Emmy awards for his work in news, including an investigation into trucking safety, which went all the way to U.S. Senator Dianne Feinstein. He is also a husband and father, outnumbered at home by a wife, two little girls and a dog named Cupcake. You can find him at dadmissions.wordpress.com talking about his frequently embarrassing, sometimes insightful, and often uncomfortable, admissions of a dad surrounded by girls.*

PART FIVE

IMPERFECT HERO

"It is important for him to remember failure is an option, not a problem."
- *Joe Medler, father of two sons from New Providence, NJ*

HIDE AND SEEK

Alex Finlayson, Emerald, QLD, Australia

I come home from work, pull the car into the garage and sit there for a moment. I don't turn off the engine. The radio is a low hum, I'm not paying attention to it. I never actually heard a single song on the drive home.

Through the screen-door I can see my kids bouncing up and down on the trampoline; their golden hair hanging for a moment against the backdrop of the blue sky and then falling back with them. They see my car and wave, smiles lighting their faces. Daddy is home. They come running.

I sit in the car and wait.

The sight of my children running towards me usually fills me with joy, but today it's a hot, piercing sadness behind my heart. It's one of *those* days. But the babysitter has to leave and there's only me here.

I sigh and turn the key. I tilt the rear-view mirror to my face and try to make the eyes staring back at me look anything other than glassy. The wrinkles curl up in the corners as I paint a weary smile on my face, but the man in the mirror is not convinced.

Some days I greet that man with elation, smiling at the other's welcome; more than happy, more than content. Other days … other days it is not so easy.

I step out of the car and walk into the house, leaving my bag by the door and collecting my kids in my arms. They are full of excitement and activity, speaking over each other and running sentences breathlessly into one another as they try to tell me about their day. My little girl hands me a homemade card. It says, "I love you daddy" on the front and there is a picture of me and her holding a love heart. It should make my soul soar. It's so beautiful but I fight back the tears and hold my daughter tightly so she can't see my face, whispering a quiet "thank you" in her ear.

"You're silly, Daddy."

Yes, baby girl. Daddy is silly.

I pay the babysitter and she leaves. I go to my room and remove the tie, the shoes, the shirt and pants; the trappings of a working day. I throw on an old t-shirt and shorts. I'm comfortable. I just want to sit and wallow. Sit and wait for it to pass. Sit and wait to feel better. But I can't.

As I'm perched on the edge of my bed, my boy charges in and jumps on my back. We both roll on the mattress together, my son squealing with delight. I tickle him and laugh with him and try not to let the tears fall.

My daughter is standing still in the doorway, watching us.

"Will you play with us Daddy?"

It's an innocent question, but something in her voice punches me in the gut, as though she's unsure if the option is on the table. Poor kids. They deserve better.

I think carefully. If we play a board game, I'm likely to snap when they don't follow the rules and the last time we played hide and seek I sat in the darkness with tears on my cheeks, hoping they would not find me. I know I won't be able to do justice to any elaborate games, so I take them to the front room, move the couch and lie on the floor.

They love this one. The floor is lava. Daddy is a bridge. See if you can get around the room without touching the ceramic tiles.

I lay there for an hour as they climb all over my body and the furniture. Their laughter and squeals of delight as I wobble my legs or backside, raise a smile in the corner of my mouth. I realize, with relief, it is a genuine smile. It is a happy smile. The pit is closing and I'm coming back.

I sit up. Earthquake! The kids fall about themselves laughing, running off to play outside.

I make my way to the bathroom and splash water on my face, holding my head down for a long time, breathing deeply.

When I look up, I see myself.

Really see myself.

And I smile.

Another victory.

***Alex Finlayson** is an Englishman living in Australia with his Aussie wife and 2 kids. He is a Daddy, Hubby, Writer, Blogger and Teacher. He has a website called dadrites.com and is part of the Aussie Daddy Blogger Network. And he dies a little inside every time someone uses the word 'soccer.'*

WINNING AND LOSING AT FATHERHOOD

Jason Greene, Astoria, NY

"Jason Greene," came through the speakers. I walked up the stairs to shake New York Mayor Bill de Blasio's hand and receive a Dads Matter award; an award given to ten dads who have overcome adversity to become good fathers at home and in the community.

An hour earlier my hands clutched the steering wheel tightly as I drove away from picking up our vegetable share at the local Community Supported Agriculture (CSA). I was upset my wife had asked me to pick up the vegetables because I was on a time crunch. I did not want to do the vegetable share to begin with, and getting the vegetables today meant I had to drive into Manhattan to pick up the award instead of taking the subway. I HATE driving in Manhattan. But there I was, driving away with my kids in the back seat and the aroma of dirty beets, carrots, strawberries, and lettuce filling the car.

Perhaps the reason I hate driving in Manhattan is I have a terrible sense of direction. It didn't help that my phone was dead because my eight-year-old daughter had unplugged it earlier so she could charge her iPod and take pictures at the ceremony.

The stage was set for a perfect storm of emotions: I had a dead phone, a terrible sense of direction, I was picking up vegetables I did not want, and I was about to meet the mayor of New York City and receive an award for being a good father.

And I missed my exit.

I was ready to spontaneously combust. The anger issues I constantly tried to bury, welled up inside my chest. My heart beat fast as rage rolled around in my brain. The muscles in my shoulders bounced and tightened.

I didn't want to be in the car. I had wanted to take the subway. I didn't want the vegetables sitting next to me. Time was ticking away while we sat in traffic. I felt like jumping out of the car and erupting in a loud yell.

Then my kids began to argue and shove each other in the back seat. I lost it. I yelled loudly and angrily. I yelled at them for fighting with one another. I yelled at them for my dead phone battery. I yelled at them for not being ready when I wanted to leave. I yelled at my wife, who wasn't even there, that I did not want to drive in the first place. I was a volcano. I had sacrificed so much for my family and now that something was happening for me, I was going to miss it.

Traffic began to move as the car returned to silence. I pulled off at the next exit in hopes I could turn around. I could not. I traveled underneath the expressway hoping to catch up. I could not. I finally pulled over and asked a mechanic for directions, which eventually got me heading in the right direction.

"Sorry daddy," my oldest son said after we got going again. "I'm sorry that you're going to miss your award." I already felt guilty for my eruption and his sweet words floored me. Tears welled up in my eyes as I apologized to my kids. I told them I loved them and they were more important than any award. I had already won "World's Greatest Dad" nine years in a row.

We pulled up to Gracie Mansion (the Mayor's home) just before the ceremony was to start. As I gave my name to the keepers of the list, I was greeted and adorned with praises about my good parenting. Inside, I felt like a heel; like I was an abusive parent, instead of a role model. We walked toward the backyard and got some drinks. Then I knelt beside my three kids and hugged them.

When my wife arrived, my kids told her I was mad and almost cried. I felt like I had let my family down. I felt disgraced.

I was led with the other honorees to the back of the house where we met the Mayor and his wife. The sting of my behavior still haunted me. Mayor de Blasio spoke briefly and congratulated all of us. We took a group picture and then we all walked towards the stage. As I waited for my name to be called, I wondered what my children were thinking. Were they thinking their father was a hypocrite or had they forgotten? I felt like declining the award.

My name was called and the mayor gave me a huge hug. He handed me the award as he towered over me (he's 6 foot 100 inches tall or something) and posed for a picture. I found my daughter's eyes in the crowd and we smiled at each other. Then she winked at me.

When I tucked my kids into bed that night, I apologized again for my behavior in the car. I told them everything was my fault. My phone was dead because I let it die and didn't charge it earlier. It was my fault I missed the exit. And, although they shouldn't fight in the car, or anywhere for that matter, it wasn't their fault I lost my temper. We hugged and I told them how much I loved them. They drifted off to sleep without a care in the world.

Parenting is difficult. Being a dad with anger issues makes it even harder. Uncontrollable anger has been passed down from one generation to the next in my family for far too long. I want it to end with me. Hopefully, when my children grow up and encounter similar circumstances, they will tackle the situation with ease and sensibility. Maybe my own imperfections will make the lesson of grace even more real to them.

Jason Greene *is a former actor and playwright living in New York City who now focuses his time on being a stay-at-home dad. He writes about life and raising his three kids at www.OneGoodDad.com. One of his stories also appeared in* Dads Behaving DADLY: 67 Truths, Tears and Triumphs of Modern Fatherhood.

DAD IN PROGRESS

Micah Adams, Portage, IN

I have two sons - three years old and eight months old - and I love them. I love them so much, but I yell, and I mean YELL, at them, especially my three-year-old. Not just a shout, but an all out roar. I don't snap at my wife. The rare times we argue, voices are never raised. I almost never scream at my youngest, but my three-year-old? It's bellow after bellow, all the live-long day.

I'm primarily a stay-at-home dad so my day is always filled with umpteen plus one things to do - cleaning, running errands, keeping up with a part-time photography business - all while trying to care for two very young and energetic children. Even something as simple as playing becomes an issue, like when my eight-month-old eats or knocks down his brother's trains while I'm helping the older one build said track. I simply don't have the time to tell my older boy fifteen times to get his shoes on. I don't have the patience to say, "I TOLD YOU NOT TO TOUCH THAT," over and over again.

In 2014, I attended the National At-Home Dad Network's Annual Convention in Denver, Colorado. The powerful keynote speaker was Barbara Coloroso, a renowned author who writes and talks about childcare. When she discussed discipline, one phrase stuck with me: "If it works and leaves the child and my own dignity intact, do it." I had never thought about discipline that way. Snapping at my eldest never leaves him or me with a sense of dignity and it certainly can not make him feel good about himself. The thought of my son, cowering in fear and shame, made me feel horrible. I decided I had to stop yelling. I had to change.

Later, I sat in on a session led by Stephanie Jelley, a woman who speaks about "mindfulness" throughout the world. She spoke of becoming relaxed and centered, about breathing exercises and taking time for yourself. I marked it all up to being hippy hogwash, but I decided to try it anyway - anything to stop my yelling tendencies.

I came home a new and refreshed person, ready to try out the skills I learned. I thought I was now the wise father, filled with sage advice, the envy of all other dads, never raising my voice and instead, simply whispering my nuggets of wisdom into eager ears. I imagined blissful, zen-like moments, a clean house, shoes on the right feet. I would get "Super-Dad" tattooed across my chest.

Upon seeing my son I knelt down and gave him a giant bear hug.

"Daddy has something to tell you," I said, smiling.

"What?" he asked, his eyes wide.

"I'm so sorry for yelling at you all time. From now on everything will be different. I'm going to try REALLY hard not to yell anymore." I gave him another hug, but I couldn't tell if he believed me.

"You shouldn't yell," he said, sounding remarkably like my own "scolding" voice. "It's not nice! It hurts my ears!"

"I won't. Daddy promises."

I lasted a week.

One damn week!

I worked so hard not to yell. Any time my three-year-old acted up, I would take a deep breath, count to four and be stern but not insanely loud. Unfortunately, each time I did, I felt more and more stress. My brain felt like a pressure cooker.

I finally exploded as I drove back from dropping my wife off at work.

"DADDY! DADDY! DADDY! IM HUNGRY!!! IIIIIMMMM HUUUUUUUUUUUNGRY!!"

We ate before we left the house, not twenty minutes ago.

"You can eat when we get home," I said, breathing, counting.

"I'M HUNGRY!!!!!!!!" he screamed.

This went on for about seven minutes. My eye began to twitch, but I kept breathing and counting and when a song I love came on the radio I said in low voice, "Please stop whining. Daddy wants to hear this song."

"I'MHUUUUUUUUUUUUUUUUUUUUUUUNGRY!!!!!!!!!!!!!!!!!!!!!"

That was it, I lost it.

"STOP F*ING WHINING! I AM SO F*ING SICK OF ALL THIS GODDAMN WHINING! IT NEEDS TO F*ING STOP!" I screamed at the top of my voice, waking up my eight-month-old.

I nearly lost control of the car, shocked at what had come out of my own mouth. I had just sworn at my son, at a three-year-old little boy! I felt like a monster. My job is to protect my kids from the worst of the world, not personify it. I just told my hungry kid to f'ing shut it. What kind of father does that?

There was a moment of stunned silence. Then, both of my sons started screaming. I felt like a failure. One week, I thought. One freaking week!

Is this just in my DNA, to scream and curse at my little boys? To not exercise patience? To not hold back frustration? It wasn't his attitude that needed adjusting. It was mine.

I failed as a father, a human being, biped, and biological life. Instantaneously, I became deeply depressed and wondered if I should just give up, just accept I would scar my kids for life. When we arrived home, I decided to push those thoughts aside. We went inside and I hugged my son, holding him tightly to me. I kissed him lightly on the cheek as words and tears flowed.

"I'm so sorry I screamed at you in the car," I said, my voice catching. I stared into his eyes and continued. "Sometimes, when I get frustrated, I make the wrong choices. I'm trying so hard to be the best dad I can for you, but I still mess up. Daddy is still learning." I took a deep breath, but before I could say anything else, my son spoke the kindest words I had ever heard, words I had said to him on so many occasions.

"It's okay, Daddy. You tried and that's what's important."

And I wept.

I wept knowing my son knew what mattered even when I didn't. I'm not perfect. I'll never be perfect. I might have failed in this instance, but all it means is that I get to try again. And I'll never stop trying for my sons.

Micah Adams *is a father, husband, photographer, and cyclist, just a few things he has been called. He is a thirty-year-old stay-at-home dad of two young boys and has been home with them almost four years. Despite the hours, he wouldn't trade it for the world.*

SEPARATION ANXIETY

Lorne Jaffe, Douglaston, NY

Ear-piercing screeches.

Tears like Victoria Falls.

It was the first day of camp, the first time Sienna, my two-year-old daughter, would be separated from me for a long period of time (in this case, three hours). My little girl's brain must have pulled some sort of "ABANDONMENT" trigger. I had never seen her so terrified. Her camp counselor, a somewhat stern-looking woman with glasses and a light blue shirt, held Sienna from me.

"Go!" she commanded, her dirty blonde hair falling into her face as she wrestled with my daughter. "This is normal. It's her first time being away from you. We deal with this regularly. But go or it will get worse!"

Sienna wailed. Other kids cried, but Sienna's tortured, almost guttural howls, drowned them out. I didn't feel frozen to the ground, more like my feet were stuck in bottomless tar. My knees wobbled as I thought back to camp orientation when they said some kids would act as if nothing was wrong, while others would feel as if it were the end of the world. I thought Sienna might cry, but this, this I did not expect when I dressed her that morning in a bathing suit, shorts and a t-shirt. I did not prepare for this as I slathered her body and face with suntan lotion.

Sienna's sneakers squeaked as she tried to pull away from the counselor. She wrenched herself out of her grip, scooted around her like a basketball player pulling off a pick and roll, and wrapped herself tightly around my legs.

"DADDY!" she screamed! "DADDY! NO! DADDY!"

The counselor pulled Sienna away, ripping her from my legs and my heart from my chest. My eyes watered. The general anxiety disorder-related facial tic I've had since my nervous breakdown in 2010 twitched awkwardly.

"GO!!"

Somehow I gained the strength to turn and walk out the door, letting it bang behind me, setting off a new set of shrieks. Peering shakily through the door's small rectangular glass, I saw the counselor and other volunteers trying to get Sienna under control, pulling her towards the main room as if she were a new inmate in an asylum.

Three hours. Three hours without me. Her protector. Her father. Three hours without my little girl. I thought I would enjoy the time alone, but I felt tremulous and unsteady. I drove home and watched television instead of blogging as I had hoped to do.

She ran into my arms when I arrived. I picked her up, her fresh tears dripping onto my face and shirt.

"She cried most of the time," the counselor said. "She played a little. She didn't go into the water. It's the first day. It's normal. It'll get easier and better."

I doubted it. Sienna hugged me tighter than I thought possible. I nodded and said, "Ok."

Two weeks and nothing changed. Sienna cried when I woke her up for camp. She cried as she lay in bed with my wife for twenty minutes after I got her ready. She cried in the car. She screeched once we got to the red brick building. She clung to me like a monkey, scrambling onto my shoulders once we reached her classroom. Each day was the same. The counselor tore her out of my arms along with a piece of my heart.

"Does she have something she loves? A doll? A stuffed animal? A blanket?"

Her scarf. I immediately thought of the delicate scarf dotted with blues and greens and browns and oranges she'd appropriated from my wife. She slept with "scarf." She took it everywhere, looking like Linus of *Peanuts* fame but as a fashionista. Once we washed scarf and she wailed until we brought it upstairs to air dry. We hung it on her highchair and she stood next to it, holding the precious fabric to her cheek, her free thumb stuck in her mouth. I brought scarf with us the next time we went to camp and it helped turn the tide.

"She was so much better today," her counselor said. "She cried for awhile, but it tapered off. She even stuck her toes in the water."

Sienna didn't even cry when I picked her up. She smiled and said, "Daddy!" She still wanted to be held. She still didn't want me to let go, but there was a difference. She felt safer and so did I.

By the end of camp, Sienna no longer screeched or sobbed when I dropped her off.

"Bye, Daddy!" she said cheerfully before I left the classroom, leaving her in the company of children her age, teenage volunteers, her counselor, and loads of games, toys and books.

And I felt chilled; the cold hard fact of her no longer needing me. Drop off at camp had, as her counselor predicted, transformed into a quick and happy goodbye. No wild reaching for me. No teardrops. No looking back.

She still ran into my arms each time I picked her up, still buoyed my spirits with a happy yell of, "Daddy!" when I entered the classroom, but my little girl could not wait for camp, music, snack, and the pool.

One day, right before the end of camp, I stood there after Sienna darted into her classroom with a smile and a "bye-bye, Daddy!" and I realized this was a microcosm of life. One day, the little girl who once relied on me for everything will walk onto her college campus, give me a hug, a smile and a quick "bye-bye, Daddy!" before turning towards the rest of her life, not looking back. And I stood staring, through the small rectangular glass of her classroom door, trembling from separation anxiety.

***Lorne Jaffe** is a stay-at-home dad who resides in Queens, NY. He began his blog www.raisingsienna.com as a means to help him battle depression and anxiety while being the primary caregiver to his daughter, Sienna. He has been featured on The Huffington Post, The Good Man Project, WhatTo-Expect.com, Medium.com and CityDadsGroup.com. Two of his stories also appeared in* Dads Behaving DADLY: 67 Truths, Tears and Triumphs of Modern Fatherhood.

BREAKING DOWN

Al Watts, South Elgin, IL

The sound that travelled up from the basement was more of a wail than a cry. I instantly recognized it as different than the regular cry that happens when sister knocks sister down or brother takes toy from sister. Someone was hurt.

I abandoned dinner on the stove and dashed down the stairs to see who was hurt and how fast I would have to rush to the hospital. Our son Ben, three-years-old at the time, lay on the ground, surrounded by his three sisters. His six-year-old sister had been holding his arm while they ran round and round in circles but, since she was able to go faster than him, he eventually lost his balance and fell hard on the carpet-covered concrete. He was holding his left elbow in obvious pain. I bent down beside him and looked at his arm. There was no visible injury. He didn't wince when I felt his arm to find out where he was hurt but he screamed in sheer agony when I tried to move it.

I was sure his arm was broken.

I sent the girls upstairs to get on their coats and shoes as I carried Ben upstairs. We piled into the car and drove to the nearest emergency room. My wife was out of town, as she has been for every trip we ever made to the ER, so I decided not to let her know what was going on until I had more definitive information.

We arrived at the ER and, as patiently as possible with a wailing three-year-old, waded through the check-in process and initial examination. Eventually Ben was taken to x-ray to see if he had broken his arm.

It was around 7 p.m., about two hours after we left the house, when a doctor came in to give me the results of the x-ray. He did not see a break, but the fact that Ben had pain whenever he moved his arm indicated a break. Fractures are often difficult to see in kids, he explained, and he referred us to an orthopedic specialist. As he left, he told me a nurse would come in soon to place a temporary cast on Ben's arm.

By this time I had been in the ER room with one sobbing son and three very bored daughters for about two hours. They were hungry. We had left the house just before dinner. I assumed the nurse would return at any moment so I didn't want to leave the room with all four kids in search of snacks. The kids watched the TV in the room, growing more and more restless, touching things and begging for food.

The cramped space, my irritation from the excessive waiting and my feelings of utter failure to fix my son or come up with a solution to feed my kids began to boil over. After waiting another half hour for a nurse, I lost it.

I told my kids to get their shoes and coats on. We were leaving.

I stormed out of the room. One of the nurses stopped me, asking me where I was going. I began trembling from the built up anxiety. Much angrier than I had intended I yelled, "We've been waiting forever for you to take care of my son. My kids are hungry. I am done waiting." And we left.

Immediately I was ashamed of the way I acted. My behavior was poor modeling for my kids. Plus, my son didn't have the temporary cast he needed. I felt my rash actions had put him at risk for permanent damage to his arm.

As I drove home, still shaking, I tried to think of how I could resolve this. I needed help. My wife, who still had no idea what was happening, was out of town. My four sister-in-laws who are nurses were more than an hour's drive away. Then it popped into my head that the mom of my oldest daughter's friend was a nurse. We had spoken a few times but were acquaintances at best. I dialed her number.

When she answered, I broke down. The emotions I had been trying to hold back so I could deal with the situation let loose. I stammered out the basics. I think Ben broke his arm. The ER wouldn't help me fast enough. What should I do? She asked if I had a sling or could go to Walgreens to get one. I said I couldn't. I had to get the kids home, fed and into bed. She offered to go get one for me.

Around 9 p.m. that evening she showed up at my house with a sling. She moved Ben's arm a little and agreed it was likely fractured. She put the sling on him and then went home. I was embarrassed for breaking down on the phone with someone I barely knew, but I was so thankful for her help.

I put Ben to bed and then finally called my wife to explain what had happened.

When we visited the orthopedic specialist a couple days later, he confirmed Ben had a hairline fracture at the base of his humerus. Ben chose a red cast.

I spent a lot of time reflecting on this situation. I let the tension of the emergency and my responsibilities as a father wear me down. I wasn't able to drum up the courage or humility to ask the medical staff to either help my son faster or watch our kids for a few minutes while I went to get some food. I made a poor decision to flee the hospital and an even worse decision to yell at the nurses. I was ashamed of my behavior and disappointed in myself for a long time.

Despite me error in judgment, this ended up being an important growth moment for me as a father. I shared the story with other neighborhood parents and they insisted I call them if I needed any help in the future. In subsequent emergencies (with four kids there are many emergencies) I have asked for help. Instead of feeling like I was burdening my friends, I discovered they were more than happy to help. They say it takes a village to raise a child. I'm glad I have such good and reliable friends in my village.

Al Watts *is a 12-year veteran stay-at-home dad to four children, ages thirteen to seven. He loves all sports, hates all spiders and would rather write than sleep. He is the President of the National At-Home Dad Network and co-creator of the* Dads Behaving DADLY *series. He has appeared on CBS This Morning, NPR's Here & Now with Robin Young, The New York Times and his daughter's Instagram. Follow him @BehavingDadly.*

MORE HUGS

Larry Bernstein, Fair Lawn, NJ

I hate yelling. I hate hearing it almost as much as I hate doing it. But I had been yelling a lot lately. It would have been nice to have someone or something to blame for it. Unfortunately, my children were convenient targets. After all, they do their fair share of childish mischief - jumping on the sofa, splashing water on the bathroom floor, and leaving trails of crumbs wherever they eat - driving me crazy. Yet, I wondered if these were truly scream-worthy events. I wondered if the problem was me.

By day, I am a high school English teacher. Some students I can reach and some, well, some are off in another place. All the kids appear to get a thrill out of how far they can push the teacher. As a veteran teacher, I know the give and take and push and pull that accompanies teacher/student relationships. There are always those students who are not interested, misbehave and act disrespectfully. My job is to keep the class on track in spite of them.

Maybe I was burning out or at least simmering. Between the misbehavior of the students and the administration's worry over standardized exams that filters into every meeting, the joy of my work was seeping away.

By the time I step off the bus and walk the two blocks home, I'm tired. I'm tired from the commute. I'm tired of trying to reach unrealistic expectations. I'm tired of navigating situations with kids. My patience is spent.

What I need at that point, what I really need, is for my children to behave, because the last thing I want is more issues with kids.

But, they're kids. Inevitably, they act up. And I start yelling.

SJ – my seven-year-old – has borne the brunt of much of my yelling. He is darn cute and can be funny and sweet, but he can push my buttons much more than his older brother.

After the inevitable outburst, I try to console myself. I throw water on my face and try to get space, slow my heart rate, and think. I play, read, talk, and do homework with my children. I'm an active and engaged father. I remind myself that everyone yells and gets frustrated. That's life.

Then, I remember my children's reaction when I yell.

When I raise my voice or make a sudden movement, my kids flinch. It makes me feel horrible. Why am I so awful? Why am I such a beast?

After a conversation about this with a friend, I decided to sit down and talk to SJ about the yelling. I was nervous. I didn't know how to approach him. I wondered if he would understand how badly I felt or if he was old enough to even talk about something serious.

I was embarrassed.

My wife took our older son, BR, somewhere so we could have some time alone. I invited SJ in to our bedroom to talk about my yelling.

"Listen, there's something I want to talk to you about." I began. "You know how I've been yelling a lot lately, right?"

"Yeah, I guess."

"Well, I hate yelling, and I especially hate yelling at you and BR. So I um, I, uh, I guess first off, I want to say I'm, I'm, I'm sorry. Do you accept my apology?"

"It's okay."

I smile. How can I yell at this child?

"I want to do less yelling, and I know most of it is my fault. But there are some things that you do that kind of set me off. Do you know what I mean?"

"You mean things that get you angry?"

"Exactly. Do you know some of the things that make me angry?" I shuddered, fearing an exhaustive list.

"I guess so."

"Well, do you want me to tell you some of them so you can be sure?"

"Okay."

"First off, when you keep making noises and I ask you to stop, I need you to stop. Sometimes I just need quiet. Know what I mean?"

"Uh-huh."

"Also, I need you to listen a little better. Can you?"

"I think so."

"What do you need me to do?"

"I don't know. Maybe, we could just talk a little more."

"That sounds great to me. I love talking to you."

We hugged each other. Again, I promised him I would try to do better. He promised he would try to be more understanding and not push my buttons. We also agreed we would talk each Sunday to discuss our relationship and how we communicated (obviously not his word).

"I think it was a little better," he told me during our first follow-up meeting.

"Really, that's it? Only a little?" I could not hide my disappointment. That week I tried to be extra patient and not yell. There were slip-ups, but I thought the improvement was significant.

I would have to do better.

SJ and I continued meeting each Sunday. One week he told me things were better, but we needed to hug more. It wasn't enough to just not yell. SJ wanted us to spend time together and be affectionate, and he felt comfortable saying that to me. This was progress.

A couple of months in, SJ gave me a good report. He told me that over the course of the week, we talked a lot, and I was mostly patient. It was the happiest I ever felt after receiving a progress report.

Yelling happens. I'm not proud of it. I know there are better ways to express anger, frustration, and disappointment. I'm doing better. I'm determined to keep striving.

SJ and I are in a better place. And he gives the best hugs ever.

I can't imagine a better incentive.

Larry Bernstein *is a father of two. He is a freelance writer, blogger, and educator. He blogs at http://larrydbernstein.com/me-myself-and-kids/*

BIG BOYS DO CRY

Tony Pitt, Colchester, Essex, UK

In his 58 years, my dad only cried twice in front of me. The first was after he was caught cheating on my mom and was explaining to me their marriage was over. The second was when his mom died.

All the time growing up, I remember him teaching me that boys do not cry. Every time I felt like crying as a child, I felt like I was failing as a boy. There came a point in my life where every time I felt an emotion and the need to shed a tear, I managed to subconsciously suppress it. I developed the ability to feel nothing, a cold apathy of emotionlessness that would protect me from ever having to feel vulnerable. Often times I would be described as cold, apathetic and sometimes just plain mean; others joked I was a sociopath, remaining calm in situations when others would have lost it, feeling absolutely no remorse for my actions no matter how hurtful, and being able to deal with the sights and smells of horrific events with the calmness of a serial killer.

The truth is, I have cried as an adult. I've actually cried a lot. I have just kept it hidden. I remember when I was nearing the end of my first stint in the Army and I had reached a point of utter despair, drinking stupid amounts of alcohol, sleeping with anyone who would have me, and just rotating from work to the bar to bed and repeat. There were times when I was so low, I would sob away until there was nothing left. But I would always make sure I was on my own. I could never do it in front of anyone.

I managed to pull myself out of that rut by finding an outlet for the little black box of emotions I had squeezed everything into. Going to the gym gave me a place for all my pent up energy. It gave me a forum to vent my anger in a controlled manner. I even got a tattoo of five devils on my back just to prove to myself my demons were behind me.

They weren't.

Since my kids have been born, they have already seen me cry three times. The first was when I crushed my toe on the foot of the sofa chasing my little girl. The second time was when I was trying to help my wife through her anxiety, panic attacks and agoraphobia while simultaneously dealing with one the worst bosses I have ever had. The third changed my life forever.

When my wife was suffering from agoraphobia and anxiety, she compensated for her lack of control over everything else by developing an obsessive need to keep things clean. She had since gained control of her mental issues, but her cleaning obsession has remained. Her anxiety escalated with the purchase of our brand new house. This was like a red rag to a bull for my wife: she became obsessed with keeping our home shiny and new. However, this made the kids and I feel uncomfortable in our own home. I had to open our cupboards using a corner of a kitchen towel just in case I left a fingerprint on the chrome handles. I couldn't cook because I might splash fat or grease somewhere. The toys couldn't be left out, meal times were a minefield and playing with play dough, felt pens or paint was a breath-catching moment. My wife knew this obsessive compulsiveness was affecting us, but was powerless against it. It made her feel terrible, but she couldn't control it.

On the day I cried for the third time in front of my kids, I made a comment about her obsessive cleaning. My wife started crying because she thought I was making fun of her. Immediately, following the drop of her first tear, I flashed back to the time when she was first suffering from her depression and had severe panic attacks. I walked on eggshells in those days in case something I said sparked off an attack. I hadn't known when to push or just be there for support, and I had no idea how to cope with all of it.

Now that she wasn't having panic attacks or agoraphobic, I suddenly felt everything I had felt in those two years. I felt every emotion I had squashed away because I wasn't meant to feel them as a man. Adding to the guilt was making the woman I love, cry. I became engulfed in emotions and began sobbing uncontrollably.

My crying shocked my wife. I don't think she had ever seen me cry. At the point where I was at my worst, my kids walked in and saw me. My son asked why I was sad.

I had no answer for them. I continued to cry. I was nervous about where this was headed. I feared my wife was going to slip back into a state of depression because of my stupid comment. I wondered if my wife and kids would think I was less of a man. Instead, they began hugging and kissing me, telling me how much they loved me.

The little black box of suppressed emotions had been emptied, giving me enough capacity for some more feelings in there. I discovered it is okay for a big boy to cry. It is okay for a man to feel and outwardly express emotions. It is okay for a man to talk about his feelings and not feel like a failure as a man.

***Tony Pitt** is a 34-year-old soldier, father of two wonderful children and a husband to a very tolerant wife. He started his blog, www.PapaTont.com in 2013 as a cathartic means of dealing with all of the pressures in life while trying to juggle the demands of military service whilst simultaneously being as good a father and husband as he can be.*

PUTTING ANGER TO BED

Benjamin Pratt, Armidale, NSW, Australia

"Kids, your grandparents are coming over. Want to help me put their bed together?" So began an interesting morning for our family of two adults and four kids. Interesting, as in the ancient curse "may you live in interesting times."

I had bought a cheap secondhand bed frame. I thought it would be a fun learning experience to assemble it together with my three assistants aged six, four, and three. They were excited, both for the visit from their grandparents and because they were going to help daddy build something. We have put together Ikea furniture before, but this turned out to be a step up in complexity.

After bringing the pieces of the bed in from the garage, our eldest, who is reasonably technical, decided to take charge of his siblings and began giving them orders: "That piece goes here."

"No, not that way around, the other way around!"

"I'll hold this here while you get the other piece."

It took me five minutes to convince him the bed ends should be put with the feet on the ground, not in the air. On this went for a while, and my initial amusement gave way to frustration. "Why won't they listen?" I asked myself. "I know the best way to do this!"

Finally my frustration took over. I told my son to stand back and I began putting the bed together myself. With nothing better to do, they took to providing a play-by-play commentary like it was a sporting event, discussing amongst themselves the reasons for every move I made. This began to frustrate me even more! Once the outer frame was assembled, next came the difficult part: inserting the slats. They were half-size slats, designed to slide into sockets on the outer edge of the frame and a corresponding socket in the middle of the frame on a rail. Doing this required a lot of patience because the slats had to go in a certain way.

"Daddy, can we pass you the wood?"

I looked over to my eldest and took a breath to calm myself. "Sure son, just make sure you pass them to me with the curve down. They have to go in that way."

The three of them jumped into action, delivering the half-slats faster than I could slide them in. Becoming impatient, they took matters into their own hands, trying to insert the slats themselves, bickering with each other about who knew how to install them correctly.

"ENOUGH! Put it down and go! Just go!"

"But Daddy…"

"No! Just go. Out of the room."

The three of them put down the timber sadly and left the room, my three-year-old daughter running out in tears, her brothers not far from tears themselves.

I fumed for a minute. Then it hit me.

What was I doing? This was not worth getting worked up over and it was certainly not worth yelling over. What kind of father am I? What am I teaching my kids?

With the wind knocked out of me, I sat for a few minutes, trying to gather myself and clear my head. I got up and walked out to find my children. The three of them were in the kitchen, talking to their mother and looking very sad.

I crouched down and put my arms out to them.

"Kids, can I talk with you please?"

They nodded cautiously, as if worried I was going to tell them off again. "I'm sorry I yelled at you. It's not your fault. Daddy got frustrated because this job is really tricky. Would you like to come back and help me again? I'll do my best to be patient. Can you do your best to be patient too, so we can work together? I can only go so fast, and the bed isn't easy to put together."

My eldest responded first. "Yes Daddy. I'm sorry I didn't listen to you."

His younger brother was next. "Sorry Daddy, we just want to help."

Finally, their younger sister, "You scared me Daddy. I sorry."

I pulled them all in and hugged them tightly, relishing the moment. I had hurt my children's feelings when all they were trying to do was help me. I felt like a real jerk for doing so, but in that moment, I knew they had forgiven me for my rash outburst. We spent the next half hour assembling the bed. When we finished, the kids hugged me.

"We did a good job Daddy."

I bent down and gave each of them a kiss. I was proud of my kids, not just for their willingness to get involved and learn, but also for their resilience and love.

"Yes, we did. You were very good helpers and I appreciate you all. Thank you."

Proud as punch, they left the room to go and make some craft to show grandma and granddad.

It isn't enough to simply realize when we're in the wrong and when we have overstepped the boundaries. We need to turn from our anger, to apologize and to try to make things right. If we don't model it for our kids, where will they learn it? If we don't love our kids enough to admit our mistakes, what kind of fathers are we? Put anger to bed. That's where it belongs.

Benjamin Pratt *is a stay-at-home father of four who hails from rural Australia. Happily married to his high school sweetheart since 2004, he is passionate about helping men to be the best dads that they can be. In his spare time (hah!), he is studying to become a Baptist Pastor and volunteers as a Dadmin for Becoming Dad at http://becomingdad.com.au/.*

LIKE NAILING JELL-O TO A TREE

Hogan Hilling, Crestline, CA

Recently, I was watching a documentary about teenagers. The reporter asked a seventeen-year-old teenage boy abandoned by his alcoholic and drug addict father at the age of two, "If your father was here sitting in front of you, what would you say to him?"

Without hesitation he replied, "Why were alcohol and drugs more important than me?"

I am proud I made the choice to be involved in every aspect of my children's lives from the day they were born so they would never say this about me. However, I was not the perfect dad. No man is, because fatherhood is a learning process and mistakes are inevitable. I admit it, I made many errors in judgment.

There is no one-size-fits-all formula for fatherhood. The dynamics of every family are different. Each child is hard-wired differently, but the challenge is to find the best possible methods to teach each child to become a responsible and productive adult.

One thing I felt I did correctly was staying true to my ethical values. I worked hard to instill a good value system and code of conduct. I believe life is about choices and the choices I make, make me. I held them, and me, accountable for our choices.

These standards were put to the real test when my boys became teenagers.

A friend once told me that raising a teenager is like nailing Jell-O to a tree. He was absolutely correct. (For therapeutic reasons, during the teen years I nailed a box of Jell-O to a tree in my backyard. It felt good!)

The teenage years are a handful. Biological changes occur in the body and mind. There is a lot of peer and social pressure. Sometimes the teen develops a distorted view of life as a result. Mark Twain once wrote,

"When I was a boy of fourteen, my father was so ignorant I could hardly stand to have the old man around. But when I got to be twenty-one, I was astonished by how much he'd learned in seven years."

Teenagers are very impressionable, particularly to influences from their peer group, and there is not a lot a father can do to prevent other people from becoming a bad influence. It is a very helpless feeling.

When my oldest son was twelve, I noticed some significant behavioral problems. I thought and hoped it was just a phase that would run its course and resolve itself. It did not. I consulted a therapist, who suggested my son and I attend therapy together. My son attended the first two with his mom and I in attendance, but then both his mom and he refused to continue. The behavior and attitude got worse.

The day I caught him red-handed with an illegal drug in his possession, almost placing his younger brother's volleyball career in jeopardy, was the day I said enough. I confronted him about all the behaviors that were destructive to him and those who loved him. I attempted to convince him to consider how his actions affected him and others, but his mind was elsewhere. My patience grew weary. I strongly requested he attend therapy and adhere to the values I modeled and taught him. He chose not to cooperate. Today, at age 26, my oldest son continues to flounder through life and blame others and me for his misfortunes.

I am sad and disappointed he chose drugs over his family and a healthy relationship with me. What pained me even more was the presumption by other people, even relatives, that my son's actions were somehow my fault and that he is the victim of a bad childhood and parental abuse.

One example was from one of my ex-wife's friends, who mailed a letter to me, in which he wrote, "Your son needs help. He is lost and confused. Do you want him to grow up like you did-never knowing/having a dad? I don't think you want him to be hollow inside like you."

I was a stay-at-home dad throughout most of my son's pre-adult life. I played with him, cared for him, helped with his homework and tried to instill the values I felt he needed in order to become a successful adult. All three of my boys grew up in the same environment with the same dad.

The two younger boys are living productive, responsible lives. I sincerely believe I am not the cause of my adult son's choices and destructive behavior.

During this stressful time, I attended therapy and ALANON. Through therapy I began to accept that my oldest son's troubles and woes are a result of his actions, not mine. I did my best to teach him right from wrong. It is his choice to live his life this way. It is his responsibility, as an adult, to find his way back to living a functional, constructive life.

Saying no to my son and holding him accountable has been one of the most painful decisions I have had to make as a father. It does not diminish my love for him, though. I look forward to the day we can again be father and son.

If he drummed up the courage to sit in a room with me, what would I say to him?

"Why were alcohol and drugs, more important than me?"

***Hogan Hilling** is a dad, motivational speaker, and award-winning author of five parenting books. As a well-respected voice on involved fatherhood, Hogan has conducted hundreds of seminars for moms and dads, appeared on Oprah, The Story of Fathers & Sons Documentary, ABC's Story of Fathers and Sons, NBC's The Other Half and Unsung Heroes and has received the California Courage to Care Award. Follow him @TheDadGuru.*

CUDDLE ME

Oliver Cain, Bristol, SWE, UK

It has been a long, exciting day, but my two children have hit a wall and so have I. My five-year-old daughter has reverted to punching her bed and refusing to sleep. My six-year-old son has started making funny noises. Luckily, my wife and I are both home and we make the decision to divide and conquer: she with my daughter and I with my son.

As I'm lying in bed with my son, becoming frustrated with trying to get him to sleep, I start fiddling with my phone. My son starts swishing his hands around wildly and making noises. I know this well. It's his imaginary light saber. He spends most of the day with it in his fantasy Star Wars world. I love that my son is into role-play and fantasy, but there is a time and place, and right now I am starting to feel a little agitated by what seems like a lack of effort to get to sleep.

As the older of my two children (although only by fifteen months), my son bears the brunt of my higher expectations for him. I always expect him to be the "grown up one" when my children have arguments. I always expect him to be the one who gets his shoes on first or brushes his teeth without a fuss. Whenever I reflect on this, I realize most of the time this is unfair. My expectations of him at six are unrealistic.

I give it a couple of minutes but can't hold back any longer. I say, "Can you stop that please?"

He ignores me. I am lying there stewing in my thoughts, "Why will he not listen to me?" I wait a couple more minutes then say it again. By this point my tone of voice gives way to frustration. "Can you stop it please? Settle down. It's bedtime. You have school tomorrow and I don't want you to be tired!"

I am starting to sound like grumpy dad now. My son calls me "grumpy dad" for times when he feels like I am lecturing him. I take on a certain tone and way of talking, which is demanding and often causes him to eliminate any desire for cooperation. I don't normally spot it straight away, and sometimes not until it's too late and everyone is cross. Usually he struggles with his feelings. But today, he uses his Jedi powers to show me he can rise above it! My boy clears his throat as if he is about to make a big announcement and says, "Well daddy, I was only doing it because I was hoping you would give me some attention. I wanted you to stop playing with your phone. I really just want you to give me a cuddle." This stops me dead in my tracks. I'm hit with a sudden rush of guilt followed by overwhelming pride.

"Oh, I am really sorry. I should have been able to figure that out! Sometimes I just get a bit tired and distracted." I wait to see how this sits with my young Jedi.

"Don't worry dad," he says. "Just give me a cuddle. We don't always get everything right when we're learning."

Today, in my time of need, overwhelmed by my own frustrated and disconnected feelings, my son took the lead. He let me know it's okay to not be perfect. Simply acknowledging this goes a long way to smoothing out conflicts and helping us build an open and honest relationship. He reminds me how important it is to listen, even when I feel like all I want to do is shut everything down and do it my way. He reminds me that sometimes our kids don't ask for what they need in the most obvious and direct ways.

I am proud my little Jedi searched inside himself to discover the force: patience, compassion and wisdom. It is a great feeling to know how well he understands and even better to know he accepts me for who I am.

Again, it is made clear to me that when I open up to our kids, they can be my greatest teachers.

***Oliver Cain** is the primary caregiver for his five-year-old daughter and six-year-old son. He works and volunteers part-time around school runs, housekeeping and all the other stuff being a dad requires. He is also a content contributor and Administrator on the www.BecomingDad.com.au Facebook Page.*

PART SIX

THE GOOD, THE DAD AND THE UGLY

"As much as those tender moments that we have with our families mean to us, what has equal meaning to me are the journeys and the struggles that lead up to those moments."
- *Shannon Carpenter, father of three from Lee's Summit, MO*

AS THE BALL ROLLS

Francis Linardo, Knoxville, TN

So yeah, t-ball.

Wow.

I never played organized sports as a kid. My first experience was my senior year in high school. The track team needed a pole-vaulter. I was the only idiot to volunteer. I obviously survived, but had a few close calls. Anyway, now I have to get involved in this stuff because Frank is trying a myriad of sports for that well-rounded foundation before we turn our laser focus on building his pro golf career.

But man, t-ball …

Eight kids standing on the infield as one kid stands at the plate and hacks at the ball set on a tee.

Try to imagine ye old Scotland at the time of William Wallace. Gas powered mowers are centuries from invention. The trusty scythe was the implement of choice. A grizzled old farmer works his share crop on the edge of the Scottish coast on a piece of link land: so named because it linked the inland with the beach, later deemed so bad for farming or grazing, people built golf courses on it instead; hence St. Andrews and links golf.

Hoping to avoid eviction by the lord or knight of the manor, the farmer swings to and fro his scythe, desperate for a decent crop yield. He can't stop. He's working to pay the man. Gnarly hands struggle to hold the scythe in the freezing summer winds (yes, summer) and ocean mist. A two-handed device, gangly and lethal that scythe was. Not lethal to the grass but to the person wielding it. Mind you this was a lawn implement.

That almost compares to the way four-year-old kids swing the bat at a ball perched on a tee. The ball is in no danger. Ever. It is the tee for which we weep.

You can almost feel the pain of the tee as the blows rain down upon it, while the ball sits safely in the holder or gently falls to the ground and rolls a few feet away. If the ball does manage to leave the tee, another natural phenomenon is cast into motion - *jugis de Gnati,* or running of the child. Eight or nine undersized kids wearing oversized t-shirts, ball caps, and mitts, reflexively run at the ball as it leaves its protective habitat atop the tee. Every once in a while, a rare sighting occurs when the child who just bludgeoned the tee, causing the ball to be set in motion, also chases it instead of running to first.

Jugis de Gnati also requires that each child throw him or herself onto the child who actually trapped the ball under his/her person. This *Canem Cumulus,* or dog pile, takes place regardless of the time that has elapsed from the ball being trapped by the original child and the final child reaching said dog pile. In other words, if a kid has to run from the outfield to get a ball hit to the pitcher, so be it. That child will run the entire distance offering him or herself to the top of *Canem Cumulus* upon completion of the journey.

The true heroes of this little social experiment called t-ball are the coaches. God bless these crazy bastards. What drives these men and women to sign up for this? What do they get out of it? I'm not seeing it. But again, God bless 'em. Someone has to do it.

I learned from last fall's soccer experiment, which resembled a giant six-kid amoeba roaming the field, attempting to assimilate the ball, to keep my expectations low. I realized I needed to try to enjoy Frank enjoying himself. He was happy so I learned to be happy with him.

The first time Frank took the infield, I was very nervous, completely unsure of what he would do. But true to his herd, as the first ball hit the dirt rolling non-aggressively toward the mound, Frank, along with eight of his teammates, stampeded toward the ball. The kid standing on the pitcher's mound was first to the ball. Poor kid. Nine kids later, including the batter, the first dog pile of the season was complete, thus signaling the boys of summer were back.

I was stunned Frank was so willing to dog pile.

What happened with the next batter was equally stunning. The ball was struck with some pace and was on an inside-the-infield home run trajectory. Frank dove to his left, glove in proper position, snagging the ball and triggering a roar from the crowd.

Throughout the season, as long as the ball had some pace, keeping it clear of the dog pile, Frank was able to get his glove on it.

We had played catch in the backyard, but I was never allowed to throw the ball in the air. Frank always made me throw him ground balls. I naturally assumed he was afraid of the ball. Turns out, the kid knew what he was doing.

In the last game of the season, the opposing coach asked some people about #9 and where he learned to field like that. Normally cool and detached during games, I could feel the pride and arrogance swelling inside me (the path to the dark side of obnoxious sports parent is short, let me tell you). But like a bad burrito, I choked it back. I let Frank's coach take him over there and let the boy do his own talking.

I did notice he enjoyed the people cheering for him a bit more then I would have liked. I'm going to have to drop him a peg or two the next time we hit the golf course. He's starting to like this t-ball thing way too much.

I just hope it doesn't mess up his golf swing.

***Francis Linardo**, originally born and raised in Mays Landing, NJ with his five sisters and two brothers, now lives in Knoxville TN with his wife Tracy, son Frank and daughter Anne Marie. He retired from the United States Air Force in 2009 to be a stay-at-home dad. Find more of his writing at www.franknfran.com.*

DISTRACTIONS

Mike Andrews Jr, Somerset, NJ

Summer was over and it was my first week alone with my then two-year-old son, Ben, while my other three kids were in school. I had grown accustomed to the older kids keeping me busy playing, cooking and cleaning. I had also grown accustomed to them helping keep an eye on Ben. My complacency would turn into tragedy.

By the second day home alone with just the one toddler, I ran out of ideas to entertain ourselves, so we watched TV. He was enjoying a show, so I thought I could get on my computer for a little bit. It was in the same room as the TV, so I figured I could keep an eye on him while I scrolled through my newsfeed on Facebook.

I don't know how long I messed around on Facebook, but I heard the laundry stop so I went into the laundry room to fold the clothes. About five minutes later, I went back into the living room and sat right back down at the computer. I didn't even check on my two-year-old, I just went back to typing a comment, assuming he was still watching TV. My friends were discussing Fight Club; obviously I had to join in on the conversation.

A moment later, I heard a blood chilling scream from upstairs. I jumped from my seat and turned to see my son, crying at the top of the stairs of our split-level home; blood steadily dripping from his hand as he stumbled his way down to me. I ran up and grabbed him, noticing he had a deep cut between his thumb and index finger. I could see his white bone inside the cut as blood shot out, as if from a small squirt gun. I thought back to all those cop/war/medical dramas I've watched and I put pressure on it, praying it was what I was supposed to do.

I started running through the house looking for something to wrap his hand in when I saw an apple sitting in the living room with the sharpest knife we own stuck through it. I immediately realized what had happened. We had just finished lunch before sitting down to watch TV and, after I cleaned up, I had left the knife I had used sitting on the counter instead of putting it away in the drawer.

After running around for a minute as the blood was dripping and spraying everywhere, I got my head together and found a new roll of paper towels and an Ace bandage. I wrapped his hand in it to stop the blood from dripping everywhere.

He was still crying, harder than he ever had; the kind of crying where he stopped breathing for a few seconds in between waves of wailing. As I tried to soothe him and figure out what to do next, I couldn't stop thinking about all those parents I heard about as a kid who walked away from their babies for two minutes and next they knew, the kid was in a well or kidnapped or attacked or any other tragedy that can take your child from you forever.

I rushed him to the van and strapped him into his car seat. As I sped down the street toward the hospital, he went quiet. I feared the worst. I glanced back and realized he was only asleep, the trauma apparently tiring him out. For the rest of the drive I had one hand on the wheel and one on his chest, making sure he was still breathing.

I could not stop thinking about what could have happened. I kept imaging the worst scenario. He could have died while I wasn't looking and I was too "busy" to check on him. I was too lost in my own world to even notice my child was about to stab himself with a knife. I felt numb.

Fortunately he missed all the important stuff and just needed stitches. My son was okay, but I was not. I kept thinking I was a bad father and that maybe I wasn't cut out to be a dad. I wondered what would have happened if he had died. I saw the cops arresting me, thinking I had stabbed him, my wife going emotionally and financially bankrupt, my kids growing up believing their dad had killed their little brother, fear and mistrust following them for the rest of their lives. I saw my whole family's future destroyed all because I had to make one more comment to let all my friends know how much I liked the movie Fight Club.

When I had calmed down somewhat and thought through the incident more clearly, I realized being a good father did not mean just being in the same room with my toddler. It meant interacting with him no matter how bored I became. It meant keeping him close, even when I had to leave the room. It meant always knowing the dangers around him. It meant showing him how much I loved him at all times, even when he did something he should not be doing.

It meant being a dad even at those times I would rather be distracted.

Mike Andrews Jr. *has been an at-home dad to his four kids since March 2012. He enjoys sharing his love for Star Wars and other geeky things with his kids. He blogs about being a dad on his blog www.geekdaddio.com and on the National At-Home Dad Network Blog.*

POOP ON A PLANE

Alex Finlayson, Emerald, QLD, Australia

We were on the last of three eight-hour flights on our journey home to Australia after an epic six-week adventure to England. We'd had an absolute ball. "RatGirl," my 18-month old daughter, was spoiled rotten by my family and she behaved like an absolute angel the entire time.

We were about two hours from landing in Brisbane when my little girl, who was sitting on my lap, suddenly gave me 'that look.' She started to grunt and turned a dangerous shade of purple, which was soon followed by an all-too-familiar aroma. I turned to the Missus, who was doing a wonderful job of pretending to be asleep, and grabbed the diaper bag from under her seat. With bag in hand and girl under arm, I stood up in the close confines of cattle-class and headed to the toilet. Occupied. I turned around and headed to the rear of the plane, trying my best not to bash people in the head with the diaper bag, or worse, RatGirl's backside, which was beginning to exude a very potent odor.

Finding the toilet in the rear of the plane unoccupied, I squeezed in with my little girl and the diaper bag, snapping the door shut behind us. Airplane toilets are not the most spacious things in the world, it has to be said. I pulled the changing table down (changing table is the laughable term they use for the piece of bouncy cardboard attached to the wall for the purposes of changing the diapers of, presumably, Barbie dolls) and laid my girl down on it. I plopped the diaper bag on the sink. I set my feet against the sway of the plane, unsnapped her outfit and prepared for the worst.

I was not prepared enough.

Her poop looked and smelled like a week-old Chicken Korma that had gone through a blender and then had been left out in the sun for a few days. Worse, it was leaking around the edges of the diaper, bubbling out here and there like the Bog of Eternal Stench in *Labyrinth*. And the smell ... Dear God! I adopted the Dad-Changing-Diaper stance of men everywhere and tucked my nose into my t-shirt. It didn't help. My eyes were stinging!

I took the diaper off while holding my little girl's feet in the air in one hand. I did my best to get as much of the poop into the diaper as possible but the thing was so damn full already. I tried to close it with my one free hand but couldn't without getting poop everywhere so I placed the open diaper next to the bag and then reached for the wipes.

All two of them.

I knew I was in trouble. I was doing my best to keep my little girl on the table without dropping her butt and spreading poop everywhere, but I wasn't having much luck. This stuff was the consistency of warm peanut butter and it was halfway up her back. The room seemed to be filling with a smell that was taking physical form and tickling the back of my throat with its greasy fingers. My head was spinning. I did the best I could with the two wipes but all I really managed to do was pick off the chunks then smear the rest of it all over her bare butt. She started to get even more fidgety.

I reached for the toilet roll.

There were only 3 pieces left. WHO THE F*** LEAVES 3 PIECES OF TOILET PAPER ON THE ROLL?!

I used them.

They were very little help.

I looked for hand towels.

No hand towels.

The image of being up a certain aptly-named creek without the means to navigate settled into my sleep-deprived brain. Here I was, in a tiny toilet at the back of an airplane hurtling over the Pacific with a little girl covered in the most epic poop ever and nothing to clean her with. Time to improvise.

I took my shoes off.

I took my socks off.

I cleaned her butt with my socks.

It was not enough.

I took my jeans off.

I took my boxer-shorts off.

I cleaned her butt with my boxer-shorts.

That's right, I stood butt-naked in the middle of an airplane toilet and cleaned up my girl's poop with my underwear.

I'm not proud.

I dabbed a little water on a clean corner of my boxer shorts and wiped her with it to make sure she was properly clean and then I stood her up on the changing table. She gave me a very quizzical look.

"Doodle?" she asked, as in, Daddy, why the bloody hell is your doodle out?!

"Yes dear, doodle," I said.

She giggled.

My shame was complete.

I dressed my beautiful girl and somehow managed to keep her on the changing table while I bundled up the diaper, socks and underwear, pushing them into the waste bin built into the sink. A smear of poop lingered on the silver flappy thing and I had no other option but to clean it off … with my hand!

I thoroughly washed my hands and then pulled my jeans on before casting one last glance over the scene of the crime. There were three little bottles of smelly stuff above the sink so I opened one and sprayed it around the room. It was as effective as trying to mask the smell of a cattle farm with a small bowl of potpourri. I opened the door.

There were two people waiting.

I ushered my little girl down the aisle, now fresh as a daisy, while I followed her barefoot and commando.

I took my seat and ordered a beer.

"Oh, I'll have a glass of wine, please," said the Missus, who had miraculously just woken up.

RatGirl promptly fell asleep as though nothing had happened and I sank into my seat for the rest of the long flight home.

Alex Finlayson *is an Englishman living in Australia with his Aussie wife and 2 kids. He is a Daddy, Hubby, Writer, Blogger and Teacher. He has a website called dadrites.com and is part of the Aussie Daddy Blogger Network. And he dies a little inside every time someone uses the word 'soccer.'*

FROZEN

David Blackwood, Jackson, TN

Terrified.

Helpless.

One of those moments in time where the seconds seem like hours and every detail is seared into your memory. That's what it was like to hold my lifeless child.

The kids were playing around the living room. Supermom was starting dinner. I was talking with the grandparents who had just brought the children home from Night at the Museum 3. They said it was a good movie by the way.

At some point we realized the youngest of our four girls, 18-month-old "Lady Bug," was acting strangely. She had been crawling around the floor on all fours and now was beside the couch with the top of her head against the side of the couch. It looked like she was crawling forward, ran into the couch and had just frozen there. Maybe she was looking at something on the ground or maybe she had something in her mouth. I tried to get her attention.

"Lady Bug… Look at Daddy. What do you have?"

Nothing. She wasn't moving.

"Lady Bug."

Still frozen.

I walked over and picked her up so I could see what she was doing or trying to secretly put in her mouth. Her arm was rigid, drawn into her chest. Her eyes were wide and her mouth was half open, but she was frozen. That look still haunts me.

She wasn't clawing at her mouth or throat or making any choking sounds. She just had this blank, wide-eyed expression on her face. Her lips were turning blue and her expression wasn't changing. She had to be choking was all I could think.

I turned her face down and held her at a downward angle while doing the baby Heimlich. My wife rushed over saying, "Lady Bug, Lady Bug!" Maybe it was me saying her name that froze her. Who could tell?

Supermom smacked her on the back, trying to dislodge whatever was stuck. It wasn't working and she was starting to turn really blue. Her face had the same vacant expression. I thought I might be losing one of them: sitting in my arms and slipping through my fingers.

Grandma had 9-1-1 on the cell phone and was hysterically trying to give them the address. All I could think was they would get here too late. They would take this limp child into a blinking box on wheels and I wouldn't see her alive again.

I decided to see if I could dislodge the obstruction. I reached a finger into her mouth along the inside edge and to the back to make sure she hadn't swallowed her tongue or remove whatever was blocking her throat.

Then, suddenly, she let out a little bit of air and, after a few pats, she started to cry. Nothing came up and her cry was strong and clear, but she was disoriented. Lady Bug was still not herself. Supermom clutched her and I realized the other girls had run to their room crying. The panic of the adults had scared them. Lady Bug was getting more and more energy back but, with nothing obviously wrong, we were worried.

I couldn't let go of the feeling that I was losing her. Tears streaked down my face as we sent the older three back to the grandparents and the baby and Supermom loaded up with me in the car. Once again, we turned the flashers on and went to the Emergency Room. With four kids, we should have a reserved parking spot at that place.

At the crammed ER, Lady Bug was fidgety and quickly becoming full of energy. Talking. Laughing. Screaming at people. Playing with a plastic horse and the inside of a shoe she pulled off. Normal stuff.

When the doctor arrived, he discovered an infection in her left ear. Lady Bug had a runny nose for a few days but never a fever or any other hint something was wrong. The doctor told us our daughter had most likely suffered a febrile seizure caused by the infection. He recommended a full workup, which meant needles.

So, after holding what I thought was our dying child, I got to hold a child who thought she was dying. Blood work via IV in the arm; rectal temperature (super!); CAT scan for which I had the pleasure of holding her head in place during the scan; Flu test via nose swabs; Strep test via throat swabs (flashback of choking incident was a nice touch to this test); Chest X-Ray; Urine sample via catheter, which was slightly impressively done on only the second try (the secret turns out to be waiting until the baby stops screaming to take a quick breath and then shoving it quickly into the bladder). Finally, an antibiotic shot that I'm pretty sure hurt her the most. I did my best to comfort her through the weary ordeal.

Six hours later we were home with antibiotics and a referral to a neurologist, just to be on the safe side. Oh yeah, we got a package of rectal suppositories for seizures lasting longer than three minutes. I guess it beats sitting there with your thumb up your own ass.

It was around 1:30 a.m. when we got back home but I couldn't sleep. In the other room was this kid who felt like a pincushion, sleeping soundly. I was all tied up in knots from the trauma and the panic this medical emergency created for my other kids. I didn't assure them things were going to be alright. I felt awful they went to bed scared they wouldn't see their sister again.

In thirty seconds our life appeared to drastically change for the worse. I didn't want to imagine what could have been.

There are some people who hope to live forever, but times like this make me hope I'm the first to go.

David Blackwood *is a father of four girls, husband to one woman, a blogger read by tens of people, and a non-knower of sacred knowledge. He writes a mostly humorous blog (with some sprinkling of life philosophies) around the world of being a hapless parent of four small girls. Interacting with the kids and joined by Supermom, Cat, and the Diapered Dog, life is never boring. He invites any and all to join in the fun at www.Underdaddy.com.*

A BOY AND HIS STICK

Brent Almond, Kensington, MD

Instead of trying to corral him within the confines of the play area, I decided to follow my son's lead — and even encouraged him — in exploring beyond its borders. We were once again searching for the bad guy. It does not matter to my memory who it was ... but it was Shredder, in case you were wondering. I followed my boy, who was armed with just a stick. I say *"just a stick,"* but in the hands of a four year old, it can be just about anything - a light saber, a bow staff or a magic wand. Today it was a *womper*. No use looking that up, since it sprang from my young co-adventurer's search engine. I felt the tension ease as I unclenched my jaw, lowered my parental guard and let Jon and his imagination be our guide.

Less than an hour before, he'd had yet another mealtime meltdown, intensified by a long weekend of play and compounded by relentless flurries of pollen, exhausting non-stop sniffling and constantly watering eyes. After being told every five minutes to not rub his eyes, and to blow or wipe his nose, he had grown weary of being bossed around by his dads and Mother Nature.

This particular food-related fit was a good reminder of what goes on inside his head — he was struggling against us setting boundaries and wanted to be in charge, if only for a moment. It was also a good reminder that logic doesn't always play a part in his thought process.

The specifics of the meltdown are also not important ... but it involved the continued smashing of a peanut butter sandwich, in case you were wondering. It also involved the smashed half sandwich being thrown away, leaving a perfectly intact half — one which my wailing child could not be convinced to eat because, obviously, he wanted the mangled one in the garbage.

His teachers had told us he was still struggling to grasp the concept of "if/then" as he was still deeply entrenched in the "all/now" way of thinking.

Certain he was exhausted and had no spark of energy left, I offered up a trip to the park, if only for a change of scenery and mood. I was sure I saw his eyes droop and head nod at one point during the winding drive through the woods to the park. But, like a self-charging battery, he was revved up to go the minute we stepped out of the car.

After the requisite round on the merry-go, a quick trip up the rock-climbing wall and down every slide, we set off in search of our evildoer, armed only with a dirty stick and Jon's steely resolve. We also had to find one for me.

No, that one's too short. That one's too dirty. That one's too crooked ... There Daddy. Get that one!

No buddy, that's a log.

Once we were both brandishing suitable wompers, we continued to walk — past a big, muddy puddle, pretending it was a swamp, across a dirt path covered in caterpillars, and around several felled logs. I astounded my traveling companion by jumping up and catching a dried vine hanging from a tree. Breaking it in half, this enabled us both to have even longer, more whip-like wompers. While infinitely cooler than our previous weaponry, I soon had to make these shorter as they kept getting flung around and endangering the wheels of oncoming cyclists as well as my shins.

We stopped and looked up at the sky, marveling at how tall the trees were. We knelt and made a path for the caterpillars to cross through the dirt, pausing in search of a helicopter buzzing behind the forests' canopy, which we concluded was a prehistoric mosquito.

I was thoroughly enjoying this adventure, dropping the tether altogether, willing to let it go as far as he wanted to go. As far as we *could* go.

But then, as we looked up ahead, and I wondered aloud if what's-his-name was behind the bridge crossing over the creek, Jon stopped.

Suddenly my heroic halfling sensed the scope of our trek, declared we had gone too far from the playground and we needed to go back.

So I complied and we turned around to retrace our steps. We glanced at the worms still crossing their dirt path, threw our wompers into the woods as far as they could be flung, and trudged through the big field of clover separating our journey from the playground. At his behest, we stopped for a few minutes to sit and dig some dandelions out of the earth so he could give me a flower before racing the rest of the way to the car.

I had begrudgingly suggested this outing, hoping it would be prevented by sleep, or fearing it would end in tears. Instead, it entailed a few minutes of freedom — freedom for my son from the rules and limitations of his very tall, strict world; and freedom for me from the stress of being so tall and so strict.

And though it's not vital to this tale, we never did catch the bad guy. He's still out there, lying in wait for a brave, wandering pair to discover him … in case you were wondering.

***Brent Almond** is a graphic designer, writer, husband and father. He combines all of these on his blog www.DesignerDaddy.com which was recently honored as a BlogHer14 Voices of the Year. More of Brent's writing can be found on The Huffington Post, The Good Men Project, The Parents Project, and Fandango Family. He also serves on the board of Rainbow Families DC, an organization that supports LGBT families. Brent lives in the Washington DC metro area with his husband, five-year-old son, and their pre-Obama Portuguese Water Dog.*

THE HAUNTING

Mathew Lajoie, Sault Ste. Marie, ON, Canada

"No! No! Stop! Ahhhhh don't!" shrieks our four-year-old son. Although his monitor sits beside our bed, his voice resonates loudly through the ductwork into our third floor bedroom. The sound of gripping fear in his voice causes my chest to tighten with lost breath as my wife and I scramble, kicking the heavy down blanket that enveloped us, to the foot of the bed.

My wife arrives at the top of the stairs first. I follow behind her thumping my clammy bare feet against the cool hardwood floor. Gripping the doorjamb, I swing myself into the landing and proceed to descend the staircase on pointed toes.

Part of me knows that my son is physically safe, but I am deeply troubled by the sounds coming from his bedroom. On many occasions he has talked in his sleep; a byproduct of the racing mind of a four-year-old, but this is utter terror bellowing from his innocent lips. He is in a dark place.

I arrive in his bedroom. My wife has already switched the lights on and is standing at his bedside. She removes his sweat-soaked blankets and lifts him into her arms.

His pajamas are saturated from head to toe and hug every contour of his little body. He is shaking and continues to bawl as my wife runs her fingers through his hair.

"Cash! Cash! Buddy wake up!" I scream frantically. Sitting across from him on his bed I desperately try to get his attention.

He is staring through me. With wide, red-rimmed, dripping eyes, he looks at my face but does not see me. My wife holds Cash tighter to her chest as he thrashes his legs and thrusts his hips.

I continue to call to him, but get the same result. My comfort falls on deaf ears. Walking Cash around the room in her arms, my wife begs him, "Tell us what's wrong. Use your words. Please!"

My heart breaks for him.

He shrieks and convulses until his fear subsides.

After fifteen minutes, calm is restored. My wife and I change his clothes and sheets and tuck Cash back into his bed. He does not say a word, but settles deep into his pillow and drifts off to sleep.

I feel relieved but I am puzzled. What was he going through? Why wouldn't he wake up? Can I prevent this from happening again?

My wife and I return to our bedroom and apprehensively put our ears to the baby monitor speaker. We do not sleep for the rest of the night, but Cash rests soundly.

In the morning, Cash does not remember the episode. He is only confused about how his pajamas changed overnight.

This was the first of several instances where Cash experienced night terrors.

Recognizing he was having night terrors was the first step toward our family coping with what he was going through. The primary characteristics that allowed us to differentiate what he was experiencing from typical nightmares were:

- It was occurring between 1.5 and 3 hours after he went to sleep (non-REM sleep).
- We could not wake him – it is more difficult to rouse someone out of non-REM sleep.
- He did not recall the episode.

Cash's night terrors were more traumatic for us as parents than they were for him. The nature of night terrors and the inability to soothe or comfort is extremely upsetting. I feel for any parent who has to witness their child going through one.

How did we learn to help our son through his night terrors?

- We comforted him and protected him from anything that may hurt him if he was thrashing.
- Did not try to wake him, but provided a calming atmosphere when he did wake so he could comfortably fall back to sleep.
- We learned to be patient and recognize the night terror would subside.
- Sometimes we moved Cash to a room with a cooler temperature to help his body rouse out of deep sleep.

Children can experience one or several nights of night terrors. Luckily, our son's night terrors have subsided. And, although they do not have an adverse effect on him, I hope they never return.

***Mathew Lajoie** is a writer and stay-at-home-dad. He lives in Toronto, Ontario with his wife, son, and dog and is the creator of the blog YOUAREdadTOme.com. Mathew is also a contributing writer for The Dad Network. Aside from writing and being a family man, Mathew enjoys golf, skateboarding, and fitness.*

VELOCIRAPTORS

Art Eddy III, Stanhope, NJ

"That's right, but they never attack the same place twice. They were testing the fences for weakness, systematically. They remember." - Robert Muldoon (Bob Peck), Jurassic Park

I have two girls. One is three years old and the other is one. They are innocent little creatures, as long as I have both eyes on them.

As their stay-at-home dad, I try to make sure we are doing something fun each day. One great way, in my experience, is working on some type of craft. Whether it is making jewelry, funny hats, finger painting, or coloring with crayons, I try to keep them busy and entertained.

Since Valentine's Day was coming, I brought out huge sheets of white paper and crayons to make some Valentine's Day cards for their grandparents. We were having a good time giggling and coloring when the phone rang. It was one of my friends calling to see what weekend this year would be good for our yearly trip.

I stepped into the kitchen to take a look at the calendar to see which dates would work for me. That was my first mistake. After a few minutes I noticed it was eerily quiet in the other room. I checked on the girls to see how they were doing but they were no longer coloring on the paper. My oldest looked at me and started to giggle. I knew something was up. I went over to see what was going on. I saw my youngest coloring on a very large fresh, blank canvas: our new front door. I have heard the phrase "This is why we don't have nice things" before, but man, really?!

We just installed this new, clean white front door. I wanted to scream at the top of my lungs! I didn't. My youngest, Jordy was only one. She did not know coloring a door was wrong.

Still, it took all of my strength not to yell or get upset. I calmly said to her, "Sweetie, we color on paper and not the walls, furniture, or doors."

She looked at me, smiled and went back to the paper. I joined them at the table and continued coloring until my neighbor came by to ask me a question.

I feared this conversation would provide another distraction, but thankfully my oldest told me she needed to go to the potty. I quickly said goodbye to my neighbor and returned to focus on my kids. I locked the screen door but kept the front door open. That was my second mistake. I helped my three-year-old to the bathroom. Usually my youngest will follow me but this time she didn't. I started to panic. Not because I thought she was in danger, but I feared a repeat performance of her earlier artistic expression.

My fears were warranted.

While I was helping my oldest in the bathroom, my youngest noticed there was a new, very large, fresh, blank canvas in the house: the other side of our front door. As I came around to the front part of the house after helping my oldest daughter in the bathroom, I saw my youngest. She sat next to the open door, grinning at me with her latest artistic creation beside her. REALLY?!

It took everything I had to stay calm. Through clenched teeth I, again, explained that we color on paper and not the walls, furniture, doors, etc. I picked up the paper and said, "color this." I then pointed to the door and said, "we don't color that."

As I was cleaning the front door, while keeping a watchful eye on my daughters, I suddenly started to chuckle. The lines of Bob Peck's character, Robert Muldoon, from "Jurassic Park" ran through my mind. It was the part where he explained about how the velociraptors remember things. It made them intelligent beings because they were able to learn exactly when to strike their prey. Also, he explained how quiet they got when they were on the hunt. I thought of my youngest as a little velociraptor and how she knows when she can get away with things while I am tied up somewhere else. If this was a preview of things to come, I knew I was going to need to learn how to be patient as my kids continue test my boiling point.

Instead of getting upset as I scrubbed red and pink crayon off the door, I laughed. My girls are velociraptors, knowing exactly when to strike. They can't help it. They want to test their boundaries and try new things. I can't blame them for that. For me, now more than ever, it is the little things in life that make me smile, especially when it comes to my girls.

After I finished cleaning the door, I kissed my daughters and said to Jordy one of Robert Muldoon's famous lines from the film, "Clever girl!"

***Art Eddy III** is an at-home dad. He and his wife, Jess, are blessed with two daughters, Lily and Jordan. Art is a writer for www.LifeOfDad.com and produces two podcasts on that site: "The Life of Dad Show" and "The Life of Dad After Show." Art loves making his family laugh, doing crafts with his daughters, and just hanging out with his family. A self-proclaimed sneakerhead, Art also loves anything that deals with Star Wars, 49ers, Bulls and Red Sox.*

INDEPENDENCE DAY

Lorne Jaffe, Douglaston, NY

"Wanna do it SELF! Wanna do it SELF! Wanna do it SELF!" She thrashes like an angry crocodile caught in a net.

"Sienna, calm down!" I say, my frustration near boiling over. "You can't change your diaper by yourself!"

Poop leaks everywhere as she flails. I take a deep breath, wishing to skip potty training (we still haven't started) and go right to whatever craziness comes next.

"Wanna do it SELF! Cold wipe!"

I take a wipe and place it on her face without even asking her to say, "Please." She grabs it in one hand and starts sucking her thumb. She has a wipe infatuation of late. It is bizarre and annoying, but that's alright. Her body eases and I quickly remove the odious diaper for a clean one. Then I scrub away any poop that leaked on her changing mat, all while thinking of Sienna paraphrasing Bill Pullman's classic line from the Will Smith 1996 blockbuster film: "Today, I DEMAND my Independence Day!"

We might be a month away from the Fourth of July, but Sienna is in the throes of a sudden independence streak. She wants to do everything herself - open doors, use silverware (if I can actually get her to consume some food), touch the elevator button, brush her teeth, change her diaper, climb into her car seat, etc. Name it and she wants to do it, without help, even if she can't. Then, when she isn't able to do it because she's not old enough or physically strong enough, she throws wild tantrums that test my patience.

It's not that I don't want her to do things on her own. It's my job to teach her to be self-supporting. I think I'm doing okay, but her forbearance is as thin as a spider web and breaks just as easily.

I open the car door and immediately she starts yelling, "Wanna do it SELF! Wanna do it SELF!"

I remind her of her manners. She whispers, "Please."

I let her climb in and then wait and wait and wait. Once she finally sits in her car seat, it's a battle because she wants to buckle herself in, but she can't. I show her how it's done and explain that it's too difficult at the moment. She yells and kicks and whips her arms and torso about until I latch the buckle. Sometimes a new wipe helps. Sometimes it does not. And then there's eating. She demands to use a spoon herself to eat milk and Cheerios except she scoops up a bite or two and dumps the entire bowl on the table.

She's testing me. She's testing her boundaries. She thinks she's ready to do everything without the help of mommy and/or daddy but the slightest impediment causes some sort of toddler hormone to course through her blood causing tantrums, thrown food and incessant crying.

And I want to get away. Far away. I want to run away from my job as the at-home parent because the "Terrible Twos" are real and they're frightening as hell. I resent her for making me clean up bowlfuls of wasted Cheerios and milk. Then the guilt sets in because I know my little girl just wants to grow up fast and do the same things at the same level mommy and daddy can do them. Guilt and frustration rip through my brain when I have to clean up the yogurt thrown across the room and bathe both her and myself after she spits medicine all over the place. I've been reduced to creating toddler-related memes using an online meme generator and posting them on Facebook (hoping one will go viral) to let out my disgruntlement.

I count the minutes until I get relief when it's time for Sienna to nap ... if she naps. Often, naptime is my favorite part of the day. Is that wrong? On really bad days I count the hours until bedtime or until my wife, Elaine, gets home and I can get some peace.

Sienna is two-years-old. She is growing up. She is talking in sentences. She wants her independence day, week, month, year, life. I get it, but sometimes it gets to me. Then she'll smile and I'll remember how much I love her.

So I'll keep doing my job. I'll teach her and bear the burden of my little girl's frustration at not having the dexterity yet to put on her own clothes or buckle her car seat. Because that is what dedicated, loving parents do.

***Lorne Jaffe** is a stay-at-home dad who resides in Queens, NY. He began his blog www.raisingsienna.com as a means to help him battle depression and anxiety while being the primary caregiver to his daughter, Sienna. He has been featured on The Huffington Post, The Good Man Project, WhatTo-Expect.com, Medium.com and CityDadsGroup.com. Two of his stories also appeared in* Dads Behaving DADLY: 67 Truths, Tears and Triumphs of Modern Fatherhood.

THE LAST HUCKLEBERRY

Phil Corless, Coeur d'Alene, ID

It is the quintessential late-summer activity in Idaho, like eating corn dogs at the State Fair in Iowa or playing beach volleyball in California. My family looks forward to the warm months of July and August when we can venture into the mountains in search of the elusive huckleberry, a deliciously purple distant cousin of the blueberry. They only grow in the wild, under specific conditions, and in unique places, usually high in elevation.

Ten years ago we were lucky enough to find a good spot five miles along a dirt and gravel Forest Service road where the huckleberry bushes were plentiful and the trails into the woods seemed manageable. For the next few years we stuck to that spot. My kids grew familiar with it, being able to spot the subtle space in the trees where we could grab a branch and pull ourselves up the slope to find a rough trail that meandered further up and in. The best berries were always toward the top of the ridge, away from the road, where it felt remote, and chances always seemed good we might stumble upon a bear gorging itself on the precious fruit.

It was four years into our annual pilgrimage to the mountains when we had a scare that haunts me to this day. I can still summon a slight shiver in my spine by merely recollecting the horrible day when my happy young children bounded out of sight through the evergreens and vanished without a trace.

We were two hours into picking, some of the berries going into containers, a whole lot more going into our mouths. Our fingers, faces, and clothes were stained with huckleberry juice, a badge of honor and delight we hated to wash away. The kids were growing tired in the heat of the afternoon and I realized we had all just about had our fill.

It was quiet and peaceful in those woods. A slight breeze would rustle the leaves and pine needles for just a moment before switching off and letting the absence of sound return. There was no cell phone service up there, which added to the tranquility.

My son, aged ten, had been devoting himself to one particular bush ten feet from where I plucked my own, when he turned and said, "I'm done." That was his way, not to drag something out beyond its welcome. My seven-year-old daughter heard this through the trees, where she stuck close to her mother, and announced she was done too.

Thinking we would be back in another few days, my wife and I did not hesitate to agree we had plenty of huckleberries, both in our gallon milk jugs and in our stomachs. We gathered our belongings and made our way along the slope toward the trail leading back down to the road.

Picking huckleberries, however, is like eating potato chips. That "last one" isn't always so. As we made our way down the trail, our eyes were now keenly attuned to spotting berries on bushes that had appeared to be picked over when we first arrived. Walking down, we would stop and exclaim, "Oh, there's some big ones!" or "Just a few more!"

The kids were growing restless, so my son, being the responsible big brother he was, asked if he and his sister could just keep going. It was only about 150 feet to the van, and they could unload their berries into the cooler all by themselves.

I could glimpse a section of the road through the trees. I knew it was close. I knew there were no bears. I knew there were no people. I threw my son the keys and told him, "We'll be right behind."

My wife and I continued to pick. We were greedy for those juicy purple morsels that are so good in pancakes, pies, and ice cream topping. Five minutes later, we realized we needed to return to the van and our hot and bored kids. We started down the trail. It would be two minutes before we emerged through the trees.

That's when I heard the car. A moving car. Crunching along on the dirt and gravel, approaching slowly, then moving away. I thought nothing of it until my wife, just ahead of me, burst onto the road and immediately called back, "They're not here."

I followed, quickly scanned the van to see if the kids were inside. They weren't. Then I looked up and down the road to see if they were chasing a snake or chipmunk. No sign of them.

Fear hit me like a bullet to the chest, knocking the breath from my lungs so that I had to think to breathe. My mind went into overdrive. Where could they be?!

The car!

Had the car come along as my kids fumbled with the keys to open the back door?

Had the car slowed just enough to scoop them up and steal them away?

My mind raced wildly, goaded on by a recent kidnapping in our area of a young brother and sister.

I ran, toward what, I do not remember. I screamed their names down the road in both directions. I shouted their names up the mountainside and down into the valley. My wife was in a panic. Trying to catch my breath, I realized I had to go after them.

The keys. My son had the keys to our van. Reading my mind, my wife yelled, "My keys are in my purse. Inside!"

Without even hesitating, I picked up a rock the size of my fist and launched it at the driver's side window. It bounced back, narrowly missing me. I spun around and searched for another, bigger rock, spotting one the size of a small dog. Hefting it off the ground with both arms, I pushed it into that window with all my might. The safety glass shattered into a million pieces all over the inside of the van. We would find those jagged bits and pieces in every nook and cranny for years to come.

I reached for the inside lock and pulled it up. Immediately, the alarm shrieked and blared at an ear-piercing volume. Grabbing the other set of keys from my wife's purse, I brushed the glass from the seat and jumped in, revving the engine and kicking up dust as I made my way back down the mountain. My wife stayed behind, in shock but needing to stay in that spot, just in case the kids showed up.

Five miles down the fire road, there was a road crew working on railings. As I drove, I continually dialed 911, but service was unavailable. Finally I roared up to the flagger at the side of the road and babbled incoherently to her about a car with kids in it and did she see it and how far ahead are they?

I slowed down and repeated myself. She understood. No, there had been no car before mine. She asked, "Have you called the sheriff?"

"No phone service!" I cried.

"I have service on mine," she replied.

She held out her phone and I furiously called 911. The operator listened intently to my story of my kidnapped children and immediately dispatched a car. "It will be about ten minutes," she told me. "You wait for the deputy there. While you're waiting, tell me what your kids were wearing."

Just then, inexplicably, my phone rang. It was my wife, back up on the mountain. Either I was dreaming, or the phone coverage goes in and out with the breeze. Whichever the case, I held my phone up to my other ear, and heard the glorious words, "I found them."

Everything after that was a blur of tears and hugs and regrets.

It turns out that my son and daughter had followed a narrow deer path that branched off from the main, paralleling the road and then sloping upward to the top of the ridge. And over. Looking back at it, my son said, "I thought something seemed wrong, but I figured a path leads somewhere."

However, my panicked efforts to save them from an imaginary foe were not in vain. As my son and daughter crested the ridge, hand in hand, heading deeper into the thick forest and further from the road, they stopped abruptly because I picked up a boulder, heaved it through the van window, shattering the glass into oblivion, setting off the car alarm.

The deafening shriek of the alarm signaled to them that they were walking the wrong direction. It caused them to turn around and follow the sound. They were mere minutes from descending into a heavily forested valley, where there was no road or line of sight, or any way to stop themselves from becoming lost and afraid.

I saved a piece of the window I broke. It's in a small plastic container that sits on a shelf above my office desk. I wanted to remind myself of the positive outcome of that day. And to never forget what might have been.

***Phil Corless** is a stay-at-home homeschooling dad to two amazing teens. He's been writing about fatherhood, family, and life in the not-so-wilds of North Idaho since 2004 on his Idaho Dad blog at www.pkmeco.com/familyblog/. Seventeen years after leaving the corporate world, he now relishes his many jobs as teacher, cook, butler, housekeeper, chauffeur, and jester, as well as being involved with his son's Boy Scout troop as an Assistant Scoutmaster.*

TORRENT OF LOVE

Shannon Carpenter, Lee's Summit, MO

The house is quiet, unusual for my home. Normally it's filled with screams, yells, dog barks and the sound that comes from Hot Wheels cars being chunked down the stairs. But it is 3 a.m. and no one is up to make any sounds.

That's a lie and I know it. Not right now I don't because I'm dreaming I'm an alien refugee stranded on a planet and forced to fight for the enjoyment of the overlords. Little do they know I am planning a rebellion. It's basically Space Spartacus. I like it. I'm a hero.

"Daddy," I hear softly.

"Daddy," I hear again as the dream fades away and wakefulness comes to me. I open my eyes and I see my eight-year-old daughter sitting on the edge of my bed. She is silhouetted by the open bedroom door she must have tiptoed through to get into my bed. I glance at my clock. It's 3 a.m. This dark shape I'm looking at is either the creepy ghost kid from *The Ring* or my daughter.

"Daddy, I don't feel good," the almost-*The Ring* girl says.

I sit up in my bed. My nice cozy and warm bed. We have the flannel sheets on with a down comforter on top. It's warm and snuggly. My daughter is sitting on her knees at the foot of the warm and snuggly bed. When you don't feel good, is there any better place to go to than your parents' awesome snuggly and warm bed? Isn't snuggling right into Dad's hairy chest the ultimate I Don't Feel Good treatment? I think so.

She scoots closer.

"Daddy, I don't feel good" She says again.

I am about to comfort her and tell her it's going to be okay. My plan is to feel her head, because that always makes them feel better, give her a kiss, offer her some water and tuck her back into her bed. That usually does the trick. Was it a nightmare honey? Did you have a bad dream? Did you miss Space Spartacus?

I don't get the chance.

Immediately she opens her mouth and out comes something that surely, at one point, came from Linda Blair in the *Exorcist*. The word that briefly pops into my head is "projectile." Dear God, projectile.

With cat like reflexes I do the only thing I probably should not have done. I cup my hands together and try to catch it. Yup, I try to catch a tidal wave of puke. The girl from *The Ring* is puking. I'm playing Yogi Berra trying to pull it down for a strike.

What happens next can actually be expressed in a mathematical equation. Or simple physics, really. The velocity of pea soup puke plus the volume of the puke (squared) multiplied by the natural incline of my hands make equals a filthy glob of juiciness that hits me square in the mouth and nose.

I'm awake now.

Which is good because of course she's not done. "The bathroom! The bathroom! THE BATHROOM!" I yell as she lets go again. She is leaning a bit forward now as she was starting to get out of our bed. So was I. This time the puke misses my hands, still cupped with puke in them, and hits me square in the chest and begins to trickle down my chest hair. She lets go again and this one hits me in the stomach. We are making progress.

We both run to the bathroom. She is continuing to spew and I'm continuing, for some unknown reason, to hold a good amount of puke in my cupped hands. I don't know why I'm not dropping it. Honestly, at this point, it makes no difference. Habit? I don't know. All I know is that we have got to make it to the master bathroom tub as soon as possible.

I could have gone for the sink but I doubt that would contain it. No, this is tub puke. Every parent at some point will wonder how their child could have so much puke in them for such little people. But then, one day, you are covered in puke and somehow that question no longer becomes relevant.

At this point my wife wakes up, very disoriented. "What's going on? What's happening?" she says. She's not Space Spartacus, that's for sure. I call out to her from the bathroom and tell her that our daughter is sick, that she puked everywhere, that I could use an extra set of hands.

She walks into the bathroom and sees me. She is rubbing her eyes.

"There's throw up on the dog," she says.

The dog. The dog has throw up on him.

I am covered in puke, practically head to toe. And this is where I will let you know I am also naked. Naked as the day I was born. Naked because sleeping naked is awesome. Getting puked on while naked is not awesome. And my wife is worried the dog has puke on him. I've seen the dog eat his own poop before. I am not worried about the dog. My wife is not really a morning person. Luckily, I am.

Shortly we get the shower running. Baths are taken, nakedness is covered up. Heads are felt, medicine is given and I have washed throw up out of places that shouldn't have throw up near them outside of a certain German film genre. An hour later, beds are remade and sheets are washed. I should definitely start sleeping with clothes on during flu season.

My daughter is asleep, laying on my chest because that's where you go to feel better. That's where you go to stop worrying, to listen to stories, to forget about what makes you feel bad. It's where you get understanding and warmth. It's where Space Spartacus battles the evil overlords and their vile puke filled monstrosities. Dad's furry bear-like chest, it's where you are safe.

And occasionally, it soaks up puke pretty well. Better than the dog.

***Shannon Carpenter** is a strapping older gentleman who enjoys the occasional donut topped with chocolate. And sprinkles, yeah sprinkles. Sprinkles are the bomb. As a stay-at-home dad for the last seven years, he vows to take all comers in the speed diaper changing challenge. With three kids who have pushed him to his limits, he has learned to love, to laugh and to make really good sour cream enchiladas. Read more of his adventures at http://thehoss-*

manfamily.blogspot.com. Two of Shannon's stories also appeared in Dads Behaving DADLY: 67 Truths, Tears and Triumphs of Modern Fatherhood.

PART SEVEN

PROUD DADS

"We don't get a paycheck for being a parent. Our reward is not measured in dollars and cents. It is in the moments when our child does something we had a hand in teaching."
- Al Watts, father of four from South Elgin, IL

FOR THE LEAST OF THESE

Matt Swigart, Cottage Grove, MN

In my twelve years as a youth pastor, one of the most useful tools in helping young people grow in maturity was the short-term mission trips to help others in need. While it was a highlight of my job, it was also a challenge for my family to have me away for up to three weeks a few times a year. I am blessed to have an extremely high capacity wife who has never complained and who sees the positive impact we were making through these trips.

I was excited when I was finally able to bring my family on my annual spring break mission trip to Houston, Texas. At that time we had just two kids: Caitlyn, age seven, and Caleb, age three. It was a blessing to have them and my wife, Christina, with me to see that aspect of my life. It was also a huge asset to me as a pastor to be able to model what a healthy family looks like for many kids who, unfortunately, did not come from healthy situations.

One moment on this trip, however, has become seared into my memory as one of the most special moments I have ever experienced, both in missions and as a daddy.

Caitlyn, like pretty much every other seven-year-old girl I have known, had two, among many, areas of needed growth. The first was that she was beginning to realize she was not the center of the universe, and the second was that there comes a point where you just have too many stuffed animals in your bedroom.

One night, a couple months before the trip, her mom and I were in Caitlyn's room enjoying our bedtime routine of Bible reading, prayer, hugs and kisses. As I tried to find room on her bed, I couldn't help but notice there was hardly any room for her, much less both parents with all the stuffed animals! With the upcoming trip in mind, the wires of my brain made a fun connection.

I asked her to go through her room and put all of the stuffed animals she didn't use anymore in a garbage bag. I told her we were going to do something special with them on the mission trip to Houston. I hoped my idea would be a memory-making experience that would become a key foundation in her life moving forward as well as help her with two of her needed areas of growth.

While in Houston we always partnered with an organization called Youth With A Mission (YWAM) that works primarily with the homeless and street kids in one of the most notorious neighborhoods in the country, Montrose/Westheimer. Every Wednesday night they set up a church service called Montrose Street Reach in a nearby parking lot. After the service, they serve a meal to those who attended. Unfortunately, anyone who has worked in settings like this knows many of these street kids are forced to sell their bodies in order to survive.

Sometimes it is for bad reasons, like drugs. For others it is to buy food or rent a motel room for a night of shelter and safety. Many of the young ladies who come to Street Reach are accompanied with small children. YWAM sets up a little area in the parking lot with mats on the ground and a little fence surrounding toys for the kids to play with as their moms participate in the church service.

My plan for that night, dreamed up months before in Caitlyn's bed, was to have Caitlyn help the kids from my group who would be serving in the children's area. This would allow me to focus on making sure my group was safe and to effectively serve with my friends from YWAM. Everything went off without a hitch, which was very exciting, but in the back of my mind I could not wait for the evening to wrap up because that was the moment I had been waiting for.

We had brought the big bag of stuffed animals with us all the way from Minnesota for this purpose. I wondered if being on this trip, seeing the hurting people we had served and being a part of the discussions I was having had any effect on Caitlyn's little mind and heart. Our plan was that when the moms came to pick up their child from the childcare area, Caitlyn would give each child a stuffed animal from her bag.

Finally the time came and, as I stood in a spot where I was able to observe without her knowing, I could hardly contain the pride and love I felt for Caitlyn and the emotions that came with it. She did not just go give each kid a random animal. No, she very meticulously filtered through her bag to pull out the perfect toy for that child, the one she had been planning to give him or her all evening.

In the five years since then, Caitlyn has continued to grow and experience new things. She loves soccer, basketball, gymnastics, piano, saxophone, art and reading. I have had many moments where I have been proud of her. This story rates up there with all those others. What really sets this story apart is that this was not a situation where effort or talent helped her stand out. This was a moment more about her heart and character, which will last far beyond anything else and, without a doubt, is more important than any talent or skill.

One of the most important things I can do as a daddy is teach my children about living for something more than themselves. We as dads (and moms) need to remember our job in raising children is not just about teaching right and wrong behavior. We are not raising children. We are raising future adults. Future adults who, we hope, will always think first of the least of God's children.

***Matt Swigart** is a former youth pastor of twelve years who currently leads the MN Region of LEAD222, an international youth pastor mentoring/coaching ministry. Matt's primary ministry function, however, is with his wonderful family: wife Christina and three amazing children, Caitlyn, twelve, Caleb, eight, and Lucy, four. Along with ministry to his family and youth pastors, Matt is in his third season as the Head Men's and Women's Tennis Coach at the University of Northwestern-St. Paul. Pastor Matt and his family live near St. Paul, MN. One of his stories also appeared in* Dads Behaving DADLY: 67 Truths, Tears and Triumphs of Modern Fatherhood.

ACTIONS SPEAK LOUDER

Carl Wilke, University Place, WA

Over the twenty years I have been a parent, one of the biggest fears I've faced has come from within. It's the fear that sometimes I might actually be hurting my children instead of helping them grow into happy and productive adults. What exacerbates this fear is not seeing tangible results of my parenting right away, and often not for years later. In fact, sometimes when my kids are squabbling or misbehaving I question myself. I have tried to remain as true to my parental convictions as possible, knowing I am going to make mistakes along the way, but hoping and praying the successes will overcome the failures. As with most families, the first child bears the brunt of the parental learning curve while he or she blazes a trail through childhood. In my family, that trailblazer was my daughter, Nora.

I've had the privilege to be a full-time stay-at-home dad for the last fourteen years as our family has grown to include six children, now ranging in age from two to twenty. Perhaps the greatest benefit of being so actively involved in the day-to-day lives of my children is how close I am with them. Nora and I spent many hours together over the years building our relationship: time spent in my lap as a toddler reading books and playing games on road trips across the country; time spent as an adolescent in conversation about friends and God and boys and school and death of loved ones; time spent as a teenager teaching her to drive a car and planning for life after high school. Throughout her life, Nora has challenged me to be a better father through her creativity and determination to do things her own, unique way. At times I felt I was not getting through to her because she wasn't following my suggestions. I feared I had failed her somehow. Raising a teenager does not follow a direct or easy path. Her senior year in high school was particularly challenging because I felt she lacked direction and purpose in her academic studies and seemed indecisive about what to do after graduation. On top of that, my wife was pregnant with our sixth child who was born three days before Nora graduated. Then, two days later, she was on an airplane, moving nearly 2,000 miles away, back to Wisconsin where we had lived for most of her life to be closer to her friends and extended family. I felt emotionally drained from those five crazy days. Baby born. Daughter graduated. Daughter gone.

I figured my job as an active parent in my daughter's life was over. Throughout the next year I learned how wrong I was. Thanks to modern technology we talked nearly every day on the phone and saw each other on FaceTime several times each week. She called to ask my opinion and advice. I watched her make a lot of positive life choices even though her path wasn't what I had thought it would be. She was not going to college right out of high school. Instead, she was working two or three part time jobs, volunteering with the middle school youth at her church and singing and songwriting.

It was her passion for music that really allowed me to understand how my actions as a parent had been received. I was driving during one of our phone conversations (using a hands-free device, of course!). She told me she had worked on a new song she wanted me to hear right away. I pulled over to the side of the road to give it my full attention. She began to sing a song she titled "Actions Speak Louder":

Verse 1:

One time my Dad was walking down State Street
And he saw some people in need
When they asked for money, he said instead,
"Would you prefer to have something to eat?"
Then he went to Arby's and said, "Look here
I want to buy a ton of roast beef and curly fries.
Just to give to my friends in need
Living on the street"
Burgers and fries might not seem like much
But you'd be surprised

Chorus:
Actions speak louder than words, louder than words
And we want to make His name, make His name heard
Make His name heard
Because you know that love is not what you say
It's not what you say
Because you show your love when you give it away
When you give it away, when you give it away

Verse 2:
I asked my Dad how come he helped those men
He said, "Well Honey, Jesus would call them friends."
He took me to Seattle and there I saw
An alarming number of breaking hearts
A man was sitting with a weathered sign
Huddled in the wind and the freezing rain
Just to see what a smile could change
For someone living in pain
You wouldn't believe the look he gave
When I said he could sit inside

Bridge:
Let Jesus guide your hand, bringing justice to this land
Jesus guide my hand, and bring justice to this land
Jesus guide my hand
(Lyrics by Nora Wilke. © 2014. Reprinted with permission)

As I sat, listening to her beautiful voice and guitar, I felt so many emotions wash over me. First, I was blown away by the fact that my daughter remembered something I had done about five years ago when we were living in Madison, Wisconsin. Second, I felt validated that my actions as a parent had gotten through to her. She had received in full the messages I had been trying to send through the way I chose to live my life. She understood all people mattered and we should be kind to others, especially those who are in less fortunate circumstances. Third, I felt proud of my daughter for using her gifts of singing and songwriting to create such a beautiful and moving song. She was singing from her heart and wasn't afraid to share her beliefs with other people. I remember thinking to myself, "She gets it. She *really* gets it."

The final emotions I felt were a sense of relief and accomplishment. Relief that my daughter was grounded in her values and could recognize what was important in life. Accomplishment in the humble sense that my daughter was becoming a mature adult, due in part to the many years of hard work by my wife and me. While she was becoming her own person, I was feeling thankful in that moment and I genuinely liked who she was becoming.

While there was no "Mission Accomplished" banner flying from my house that day, there were tears staining my face as I called Nora back to tell her how much I loved her song. It was hard to put into words for her just how meaningful it was for me to know that all of the years of hard work, tears, sacrifices and prayer were worth it. I told her again how proud I was of her and how much I loved her. She told me, "Thanks, Dad. I already knew. Your actions always showed me that."

***Carl Wilke** is blessed to be father to six amazing children, ages 20, 15, 13, 10, 5 and 2 and a husband to his lovely wife for 22 years living in the Seattle, WA area. He grew up in Wisconsin and taught elementary school for six years before becoming a full-time stay-at-home dad in 2000. He blogs at www.bigcheesedad.com when not playing sports and outdoor activities such as hiking, biking and kayaking with his kids. At 6'8" tall, Carl is the tallest SAHD in America! One of his stories also appeared in* Dads Behaving DADLY: 67 Truths, Tears and Triumphs of Modern Fatherhood.

DEVELOPMENTAL MILESTONES

Dan Indante, Beverly Hills, CA

from *The Complete A**hole Dad*

Edited from the original.

Editor's Note: This story is intended as parental satire. Dan doesn't actually hate his kids. Most of the time.

My kids are now eight and six and a half. "Dan's Twin" spends two weeks at camp on her own and "Oops" has made it real clear he doesn't need me or give a sh*t about me now that he has picked out the kindergarten classmate he's going to marry. All of this reminds me that my children are not babies anymore. It's not that I miss them being babies because I hate babies. And I hated my kids when they were babies. And I for sure hate every baby that has had the audacity to fly on a plane within six rows of me.

But I do remember the unadulterated thrill I got when my then-babies passed each "developmental milestone" in their lives. Not necessarily the milestones I read about in the BS parenting books, but the ones which made my life just a bit easier. Because look, who are we kidding, the kids don't know when they've done something, you just know that some disgusting task you formerly had to deal with as a parent is now history.

In honor of my fading memory and in the hopes that I would not forget how impactful each of these events were, I thought that I'd recall the five* greatest achievements of my children's baby stage and their relative effect on my life, which is all that's really important anyway.

5. Climbing the stairs: Effect on my life (1 to 10) - 3

Not everybody cares that much about when a child figures out how to climb stairs without breaking their neck. Sure, it means you can get rid of all those ridiculous cages you strap onto your stairwell but, for you, it probably wasn't that big of a deal. For me, it was huge. When my children were 0-3 years old, I lived in a hillside house that was five stories tall and had 66 steps top to bottom. Dragging my kids up and down that godforsaken mountain of stairs turned my wife into an Olympic leg press powerlifter and I had to hear about it every friggin' day when I got home from work. And don't think she was too happy when her quadriceps got bigger than her boobs. The day my children were old enough to negotiate this residential Grand Canyon, what did we do? We moved to a normal 2-story house.

4. Holding the bottle: Effect on my life - 4.5

The interesting aspect of the "holding the bottle" trick is that, as a non-parent, you have no idea how immensely important it is for babies to learn how to do it. As a single guy, it never occurred to me that this tiny person was going to literally control every moment of my existence by telling me when, where and what time I had to turn off Sports Center and shove a bottle into her mouth. Worse, I was going to have to sit there for as long as it took, risking terminal carpal tunnel syndrome to make sure that it was angled at the precise geometric ratio to prevent her from choking on powdered milk. When she learned how to do it herself, I threw a refrigerator next to her crib, stocked it with homogenized and let her party like an infant rock star.

3. Holding their head up: Effect on my life - 5

When you bring the first child home from the hospital, you are truly clueless. This little sleeping, crapping, crying life takes over your world and you don't know what the hell to do, regardless of how many times your mother-in-law calls, screaming instructions regarding a since-disavowed parenting technique from 1971. The truly terrifying aspect of this newfound intrusion is the fact that the baby can't hold its head up. When you pick up the newborn, her head swings around like a weather vane and you're sure it's going to snap off at any second. The moment they figure out how to hold their head up and you no longer have to be concerned the next time you hug them, their head is going to roll across the living room floor, is the moment you feel like you might just be able to handle this whole parenting thing after all.

2. Talking: Effect on my life - 7

I really debated whether talking had much of an effect on me because talking is not something that happens in one day. Rather, it's a continuum. One day, your son says "mama," the next month he's saying, "want milk," then sometime thereafter, he's saying "hey, fat bald old man, give me money and buy me a car, you piece of sh*t loser." Or, like me, you've got a daughter who talks so much she develops a hernia in her vocal chords by the time she's five. But regardless of these situations, when your child utters his/her first word, you get to call the rest of your family and tell them that, obviously, you've hatched the next Einstein and that alone is worth the price of admission.

AND THE NO. 1 MOST IMPORTANT DEVELOPMENTAL MILESTONE IN TERMS OF HOW IT AFFECTED MY LIFE......................

1. No more diapers: Effect on my life - 10

Literally, I have tears rolling down my cheeks as I write this, thinking about the day I did not have to wipe my son's ass anymore. No single event could ever be half as earth shakingly important as the one that resulted in my children's bowel movements no longer being a thrice-daily part of my life. I have been known to mist up when we pass the Pamper's section of Costco. As a parent, you are forced to do things you never thought you would or could do. Nevertheless, you do them because you're the idiot who forgot to wear a condom. Still, in your wildest imagination, you never thought, never truly comprehended, that you would spend a good two to three years (per child!) with your hands sunk deep into the crevice of a small human being's ass. And when that nightmarish, surreal parental collateral damage ends, you sink to your knees like you just won Wimbledon, and thank the good Lord Almighty that it has finally, mercifully come to an end. You feel like John McCain emerging from his five-year stint in a Vietnamese tiger cage. Free at last, free at last, good God Almighty, we are free at last!!!!!!!!!!!!!!!

And then you go to Target to buy 50 pairs of Transformers underwear.

* Originally I listed ten greatest achievements but the editors of this book, or jerks, as I call them, sought to deprive you of some of my genius in order to save space for other stories. Whatever. Fortunately, my book is still in print so you can get the whole, undefiled, story.

Dan Indante *is a bitter, vindictive attorney beholden to two kids and a wife. In his latest book,* The Complete A**hole Dad, *40-plus-year-old, fat, balding, unrepentant Dan pretends to be a model parent during PTA meetings and Little League games while secretly writing hateful screeds which rage against the banality of modern parenting. Dan lives and works in Beverly Hills until the creditors from his various real estate projects catch up to him. One of his stories also appeared in* Dads Behaving DADLY: 67 Truths, Tears and Triumphs of Modern Fatherhood.

LUNCH DATE

Pete Gilbert, Indianapolis, IN

My oldest daughter, an inquisitive, energetic second grader, had pestered me for months to visit her for lunch at school. I procrastinated because the only day I had available was the one morning a week I had blocked out for me time to run an errand, shop for groceries or exercise. I did not like to surrender me time, but understood I could not continue with this selfish charade.

When I finally announced to my daughter I would visit her for lunch, she was so excited to hear the news. I, on the other hand, struggled with the anxiety of my first lunch date at school.

On the scheduled day, I nervously drove the half-mile to school, unsure of what to expect, concerned about the proper protocol involved in a dad's visit to school and whether or not I would meet my daughter's expectations.

As I entered the school office, the school secretary greeted me.

"Hello sir, how can I help you?"

"I'm here to visit my daughter for lunch?"

"Please sign in and scan your ID, then sit in the waiting area and I'll let you know when you can enter the school grounds for lunch."

For the next ten minutes the awkward silence and stares from the two secretaries, made me feel as if I was in trouble and next in line to see the principal.

As I waited and my anxiety level increased, a mom also showed up for a lunch date with her child. Apparently she was a lunch date veteran because the secretary did not ask to scan her ID. I also felt outmatched as she carried in a large bag of Jimmy John's box meals and two sodas. In addition to two delicious sub sandwiches, I imagined the bag also had one of those gigantic chocolate chip cookies. I sat uncomfortably, holding my plastic grocery sack containing only a peanut butter and jelly sandwich and an apple.

Holding my homemade lunch added to the anxiety that had started the day I announced the lunch date to my daughter. I thought maybe I was I doing this wrong. Was there some sort of unspoken protocol that you were supposed to bring in special food to eat with your kid? Would my daughter be disappointed I did not bringing her anything special? Should I just bail and go home? It's amazing how fast your brain can think of all the ways you are potentially going to disappoint your daughter for no logical reason.

After all the internal conflict taking place in my mind, I decided to stay. As I watched the second graders march, single-file, down the hallway, my daughter busted her way out of line shouting, "Daddy, Daddy!"

She ran up and gave me a big hug. She was so excited to see me. She grabbed my hand and proudly escorted me to the lunch table with her classmates.

My daughter's heartwarming welcome suddenly relieved all the anxiety and insecurity I had built up inside me.

As we walked toward the lunch area, her body language made me feel she thoroughly enjoyed the prospect of sharing part of her elementary school world with me. She introduced me to her classmates, showed me around the lunchroom and paraded me like a guest of honor.

My daughter's classmates were also great hosts. One girl told me she falsely claimed to her parents she was allergic to peanuts so she wouldn't have to eat peanut butter and jelly sandwiches. She also told me she had a "for really" allergy of feathers.

I told her I was allergic to second graders. She didn't get the joke.

In between conversations with my daughter and her classmates, I observed the innocent nature in which all the children enjoyed the thirty-minute lunch break from the classroom. And I suddenly acknowledged and accepted my existence in my daughter's Peter Pan world filled with "hot lunch" kids who ate breadsticks and peaches and "sack lunch" kids who ate a variety of items like Lunchables, fruit snacks, soup and strawberries. One girl's lunch bag included a chocolate brownie the size of her head. My mouth drooled at the sight of it. I asked for a bite. She said, "No." I didn't take it personally because I understood she had met me for the first time and our relationship was not at a sharing level yet.

In a Tinkerbell flash lunchtime ended.

I kindly bid adieu to my daughter's classmates, thanked my daughter for the lunch invitation and hugged her. She hugged back. Time certainly flies when a person is having fun.

As I beamed back into the adult world, I realized all the anxiety was unnecessary. There was no need to bring a special lunch. The visit itself was special, regardless of what I brought. My daughter was just happy her daddy was there to spend time with her and make her feel special.

And that is all I should strive to be: a loving, good dad who needs to plan the next lunch date with his daughter.

Pete Gilbert *dismissed class for the last time in May of 2011to began a new chapter in his life as a full-time dad. He taught middle school for seven years, but with two kids and a third on the way, he wanted to spend more time with my own kids, instead of someone else's. His kids provide him with an endless amount of stories, which he retells for Indy's Child Magazine.*

BEING PRESENT

Brent Almond, Kensington, MD

I don't know who first said it, but I heard my father weave it into countless sermons when I was growing up: "No one ever said on their deathbed, 'I wish I'd worked more.'"

The same struggle often plagues me when I am busy chronicling my parental journey on my blog. That's not to say there aren't some positive things to be gained from all the e-yammering I do. From time-to-time I will hear from a reader that something I've written resonated with them. Or an experience I shared was sweet or hilarious or inspiring. Interactions like those are precious to me and keep me at it. Yet, I also know our family is as struggling and imperfect as anyone else out there *not* publishing sweet, hilarious, inspiring stories about their kids.

I have also heard more than a few times, "Your son will really appreciate reading all of this when he's older."

Maybe. Or he might be embarrassed and pissed off. He will most definitely think it's lame — at least for a couple of years, somewhere between learning to read and adulthood.

As with many modern parents, I get too wrapped up in chronicling as well as planning, prioritizing, scheduling, worrying about and second-guessing any and everything related to being a parent. And as with many modern parents, I risk missing out on the most important thing: being present.

I'm not talking about being around. I can spend ten times the amount of hours with Jon as my husband does, but when Papa takes a few minutes to let him help water the lawn, or shows him how to play a game on the iPad, or calls Nonna with him, it can have more impact than an entire afternoon of running around doing errands or birthday parties or play dates or clothes shopping.

I'm not sure why it is — perhaps the onset of cooler weather or the start of my fifth year as a dad — but I have been more conscious of taking time to actually *be* with my son. I make time to watch what he's watching, to play what he's playing, to interact — and not just oversee. Starting dinner or banging out a few sentences or sketching a logo can wait a few minutes more.

One recent weekend we had taken Jon to the movies. After being cooped up in the dark for several hours, he ran straight to the backyard to get his ya-yas out. Papa had gone out with him initially, but then I heard son and dog romping and yelping and having a good time, so I got up from the computer to watch from the kitchen door. I laughed and smiled as they chased each other and barked and hollered.

And then I stopped watching, walked through the door, and got down on the ground with them. My little boy was enjoying himself with abandon, rolling around on the grass, pretending to be shot or swimming in lava or something equally perilous. He rolled my way and I saw his bright green shirt set against the still green grass. The sparkle of his blue eyes set something off in my heart. I was momentarily stilled with astonishment at how breathtakingly beautiful my son was. So I did exactly what the moment called for — I tickled him. This set off his eyes and his smile and the green and the blue even more. I kept tickling until I could get my phone out and snap a quick photo to capture just a sliver of the moment's joy. Then I went back to being present and tickling and watching his eyes and his smile and his green and his blue spin my world around and around and around.

***Brent Almond** is a graphic designer, writer, husband and father. He combines all of these on his blog www.DesignerDaddy.com which was recently honored as a BlogHer14 Voices of the Year. More of Brent's writing can be found on The Huffington Post, The Good Men Project, The Parents Project, and Fandango Family. He also serves on the board of Rainbow Families DC, an organization that supports LGBT families. Brent lives in the Washington DC metro area with his husband, five-year-old son, and their pre-Obama Portuguese Water Dog.*

PULLING TEETH

Michael Picarella, Valencia, CA

from *Everything Ever After (Confessions of a Family Man)*

My seven-year-old son's teeth were loose. All he cared about was the money he would get when the teeth came out.

"Money isn't everything," my wife and I told him. I felt his teeth. They were a bit wiggly but were not coming out any time soon, which was good. The Tooth Fairy couldn't afford a dollar, let alone two.

That winged tooth-snatcher was off the hook for at least two months.

Three months later, our son's teeth were ready to come out, but it hadn't been enough time for the Tooth Fairy to round up much dough.

"What the heck is the Fairy gonna do?" I whispered to my wife after feeling my son's looser-than-loose teeth.

"How should I know? With all the furlough days the Fairy is getting this year, there's no extra money, not even two bucks."

"Mommy, Daddy," our kid said. "If the Tooth Fairy can't afford to give me money for my teeth, can you give me money?" There's no way he heard our conversation, did he?

"Don't you worry, you'll get a dollar a tooth just like every other kid in the world," I said.

Our kid leaped for joy, ran to the bathroom and started yanking on his teeth.

"Slow down there, Indie 500," I said, chasing him to the sink. "You don't wanna damage your gums by—"

The kid had already pulled out a tooth.

"But it doesn't hurt," he said.

"But you could ruin your gums forev—"

There went the second tooth.

"That was easy," the kid said. "Look, Mommy!" he yelled, running out into the living room, blood pouring from his mouth like a vampire who had just preyed upon some helpless victim.

"Mrraaaahhhh!" my wife yelled when she saw the blood. She didn't mind that it went all over the carpet like I was yelling about. She wanted to take him to the ER.

"I'm fine, Mommy," our boy said. "I just pulled out my two front teeth."

Meanwhile, I was on my hands and knees trying to scrub his blood out of our white carpet. "Look what you did!" I said. "This will never come out."

"Carpet isn't everything," our son said.

"No, but money is," I replied. "And we can't afford new carpet right now."

That night our boy called various family members, including Grandpa and Grandma in Northern California, to tell them about his two front teeth.

"Oh boy," Grandpa said over the phone. "Did you know the Tooth Fairy is giving out twenty-dollar bills and video games this year? She might even give you that baseball glove you really want."

Grandpa made sure our boy told us how gracious the Tooth Fairy was going to be that night, all the while laughing at what he thought was a "funny joke."

"Ha ha," I told Grandpa when I got on the phone. "So we'll be expecting the Tooth Fairy from Sacramento tonight?"

"Oh no," he said. "That Tooth Fairy passed the torch many years ago."

Our son put his teeth in an envelope and shoved it under his pillow before saying good night.

"Can you believe the Tooth Fairy is giving away all that stuff this year?" our boy said as my wife and I tucked him in. "I hope she gives me a twenty-dollar bill. That'd be the best." He was so excited.

My wife and I said good night to our boy, and then trudged into our room, unsure of what the Tooth Fairy would give our son for his two front teeth.

"It is what it is," I said to my wife.

"But he wants that twenty bucks so bad."

"Money isn't everything," I said.

"It certainly feels like it these days."

The next morning, my wife and I heard our son moving. He was awake. We heard him go under his pillow and rip open the envelope he'd put his teeth in the night before. We waited to hear the disappointment.

There was no response we could make out. We remained in bed and listened for clues. We heard him moving around his room: rustling paper, scissors at work, tape being pulled from the tape dispenser on his desk.

Then we heard tapping on our door, which was only slightly ajar.

"Mommy, Daddy," his little voice crept in. He slipped into the room with his hands behind his back. He came to our bed and handed us a folded-up, taped-up piece of paper. My wife and I sat up and opened the paper.

Inside it read, "I love you Mommy and Daddy. This is for all that you do for me." Taped below his writing were the two dollars he had received from the Tooth Fairy.

My wife and I smiled ear to ear. Our son gave us a smile of his own, a big hole in the front where teeth used to be.

Michael Picarella *has been writing his family humor column, "Family Men Don't Wear Name Brands," for The Acorn Newspapers in Southern California since 2006. He paid a lot of money for his BFA from the Academy of Art University in San Francisco and he relocated to Los Angeles to make movies. Today, he still lives in Los Angeles with his wife, son, pet beagle, and* *is the writer-director behind the two highly unknown independent movies, 1 2 3 and Punchcard Player. Picarella's new book, "Everything Ever After (Confessions of a Family Man)," and more information about the writer can be found at www.MichaelPicarella.com.*

WALKING IN THE RAIN

Oliver Cain, Bristol, SWE, UK

I opened the door and the rain was pouring. It was a half mile walk to school, which could take anywhere from fifteen to forty-five minutes with my five and six year old. Already feeling agitated because we woke up late and I had not made any preparations the night before, I shunted my children through the morning routine at double speed. The clock in my head had been ticking while the tension built and pulsed inside me. It seeped out through my tone of voice and body language as I demanded compliance from my children in order to tick the morning's tasks off my to-do list at a pace that would hopefully get us to school on time.

My kids, sensing my mood, naturally refused to do what I asked, switching off in an unconscious effort to shield themselves from my impatience and stress. I warned them we would have to go fast to avoid getting wet. My son was deep in a moment of play with his Lego man, my daughter was cleaning stones she found on the beach a few days earlier. My instructions fell on deaf ears.

We finally left the house and my son began to saunter, as if on a relaxing Sunday afternoon stroll: hands in his pockets, staring into space, looking thoughtful. I could see his mouth moving; he seemed to be quietly talking to himself. My daughter, who normally hates the discomfort of getting cold and wet, was looking towards the sky with an open-mouthed smile, rain pattering on her face, the drips slipping off her nose and splashing onto her tongue. Every time a drop hit she shouted with delight, "Daddy, Daddy look at this!"

I was not watching. My brain was turning over and over, my internal monologue repeating itself, "She'll get wet and have a tantrum. We'll be late. They will be crying and have a miserable day. Everyone will think I am a terrible dad for arriving to school late with wet children."

I have noticed lately that one of my worst triggers for stress is my fear of judgment from other parents. I wonder sometimes if this is my insecurity as a dad.

I checked my watch. Ten minutes had passed and we had gone only about 200 yards from the door. I was already wet. I could see dark patches appearing on my son's trousers where the water was falling off the end of his coat. My daughter's dress had started to get wet around the neck in just the way that seems to irritate her the most.

"Come on kids! We need to move FAST or we will be soaking wet and be late."

Nothing.

I repeated what I had said, not any louder but feeling a bit more frustration creep into my tone. Three times I did this and still no response. Then, out of nowhere, my son asked, "Daddy where does it go?"

And this was it! This was my trigger! I thought, "How dare he ignore me repeatedly and then ask a question!"

I took a few deep breaths to try to calm my panicking brain. I walked over and got down so our eyes meet at my son's level and we started to talk. As he explained to me what he was seeing and asked me questions, I allowed myself to engage further instead of allowing my anxiety to take over, and we started to connect. I stepped into his world and it was a lovely place, where the most important thing right now was why the water flowed, what was in the water, and where it goes when it disappears down the drain.

My daughter came over to listen and we chatted for what felt like ages, but was probably only about three minutes - three amazing minutes.

I looked again at my watch, the stress and tension returning. I could feel my heart beating faster. Again I breathed. Now connected with my children in their world, I tried to slowly and logically explain the decision we must make together about getting to school. I said, "we are running a bit late and getting wet. If you don't mind being late, we can stay here and watch some more, but if you want to be on time we need to walk faster. I am also a bit worried that you will get wet and be uncomfortable at school."

My daughter turns and looks at her brother. "We don't like being late do we? We'll miss going in with our friends?"

"No, let's go," my son replies. "Yeah, let's go now, we'll catch rain drops on the way."

Maybe we didn't spend as long as we could have. Maybe, in a perfect world, we would have walked all the way at the speed of the flowing water. But with the power in their hands, my kids were able to make a decision that was right for them, and I was able to relax, knowing they were happy with the control and understood the consequences of their decision.

I am still learning. I am learning to keep in touch with what is going on for me in my response to situations that challenge my usual way of doing things. When my children slow or stop to notice something or make the most of an experience, I try to imagine myself in their world, full of new wonders, questions, and unknowns. Only then can I really experience their perspective in its full, magical glory. Now that I have started to share these moments with them, we have begun to build deeper connections and our relationships continue to expand in new, wonderful ways.

I have certainly learned from them and slowing down is my new shortcut to happiness. I have learned to walk in the rain.

Oliver Cain *is the primary caregiver for his five-year-old daughter and 6-year-old son. He works and volunteers part-time around school runs, house-keeping and all the other stuff being a dad requires. He is also a content contributor and Administrator on the www.BecomingDad.com.au Facebook Page.*

DEATH IN A HOT TUB

Mathew Lajoie, Sault Ste. Marie, ON, Canada

We shuffled, barefoot in the snow toward the shadowy box that peaked above the wooden floor of my parents' backyard deck. Light flurries dusted a thin layer of ice, coating the stiff and creaky aged planks.

Holding Cash's hand, I lifted the grey lid off the hot tub. Pushing it against the wall of the house, I struggled to keep my footing as melting snow turned to ice under the warmth of my feet.

I lifted Cash through the plume of steam and into the calm water. Stepping in after him, the abrupt temperature change gave the sensation of pinpricks on my skin. My four-year-old son didn't seem to mind. He enjoyed the heat.

It was a cold, December night in Northern Ontario and we could not submerge ourselves quick enough. Christmas had just passed and the days were still short. Dinner was an hour away and the sky was midnight black. The stars were out and Cash and I debated which lights in the sky were spaceships.

Spending time in the hot tub with my son is an activity I look forward to. It's a place where we can sit together quietly, jets off, and decompress. It is also a place where we have meaningful conversations because there are no television, toys or places to be.

We often talked about school, racing cars, plans we had for the following day. But on this particular snowy night the conversation between Cash and I took me off guard.

He wanted to talk about death - more specifically, the death of our dog, Chipper.

We often think of the curiosity of toddlers as ending in a humorous "you won't believe what he said": their innocent understanding of the world guiding them to a line from *Kids Say The Darndest Things.*

But we are never truly prepared for the tough questions. The unfiltered impulsiveness of children to ask about the unknown is one of the most beautiful characteristics of a developing mind.

It also creates one of the most difficult moments of parenting.

That night Cash asked, “Daddy, will Chipper die?”

“Yes. He will,” I answered after a short pause.

“Why? I don’t want him to die,” he said as he stared squarely into my eyes looking for the answer.

I could tell the topic of death had been weighing on him. I had never seen him look so intently at me before. He was anticipating my answer, an answer I had not expected to give this early into parenthood.

Cash had experienced death in our family in the year leading up to his fourth birthday but he had not asked about it.

My wife and I had taken the time to explain he would no longer be able to see the family member who passed and why we were sad. These conversations were brief and we did not go into a lot of detail. He had no questions. That is, until he had my undivided attention where he felt comfortable to talk.

It took me a moment to decide how I would approach his question. I thought about death and my own beliefs. I am not a religious person and often think about mortality myself. I have moments of spirituality but am unclear about what waits for us on the other side.

Sometimes I envy those who place faith in a higher power to accept them in death.

As muddled as my thoughts were about death, Cash *needed* my answer.

That night I looked into my son’s eyes and decided not to talk to him about death, but to tell him about life instead.

I told him death is a certainty in life and this inevitable truth should not sadden him. Seize the moments you have in life with Chipper, and the ones you love, and enjoy them.

Tell him you love him.

Show him you love him.

Treat him well while he is with us.

Make the best of your time with Chipper and create vivid memories that will survive his time on earth.

Do not let the presence of death in life taint your experiences with those you love.

There will be a day when Chipper is not with us. I don't know when that day will be. Let's make the most of his life.

When I finished, Cash just stared at me and said, "okay, daddy." I thought maybe my words didn't satisfy him and he still carried around questions unanswered. However, it was his actions the following days that spoke beyond his brief response.

Our conversation must have resonated with him. Since that December day in the hot tub, Cash has not missed a moment to tell Chipper, my wife or myself that he enjoys the time we spend together and that he loves us.

And I have not missed a moment to show him that love back.

Death is a difficult topic to discuss with our children. Our answers are lasting and impactful on not only how they view mortality, but also life. I hope my son carries with him my lessons and continues to talk to me about whatever is weighing on his mind (whether it's *in* or *out* of the hot tub).

Mathew Lajoie *is a writer and stay-at-home-dad. He lives in Toronto, Ontario with his wife, son, and dog and is the creator of the blog* YOUAREdadTOme.com. *Mathew is also a contributing writer for The Dad Network. Aside from writing and being a family man, Mathew enjoys golf, skateboarding, and fitness.*

SAYING GOODBYE

Matthew Green, Los Osos, CA

Children change so much, so quickly. They are constantly growing, learning, and becoming different people. Unfolding, I started calling it. Like an enormous piece of paper art, all folded up in a cute little package. And, every so often, they unfold a little bit. If we are not paying attention for just a minute, they have unfolded a lot; doubled their size if we look away long enough. Here is this different person now: the same piece of paper, the same work of art, but unfolded some more. They can now poop on the toilet, they can walk, they can read. Some of us weep because the old them is now gone. Suddenly they're not a baby or a toddler or a little kid. They have unfolded into the next version of themselves.

I remember crying one night. I hardly cry but when I do, it's normally over something silly, often inexplicable and alone. I wept over the young sycamore tree I had planted with Sophie and my kid sister to replace the apple tree Sophie and I used to sing ring-around-the-rosie until we were dizzy, then lie on our backs, head-to-head, and giggle at the misty Los Osos sky. The tree that was our hummingbird Lou's lookout perch, jutting tiny but powerfully at the sky on the top branch; the tiny bird that used to perch himself six inches in front of me when I was writing or smoking a cigar that smelled really good. The apple tree was blown down in a horrible windstorm, split right in two and left, sad and broken, in our backyard. Sophie had cried so much, her climbing and ring-around-the-rosie dizzy tree gone forever, only appearing on occasion to burn sweetly in our brick fireplace on cold spring nights. But I wept over the new sycamore, the great filler-in of riverbeds, because Sophie had turned five and lost the baby fat on her face and was starting school and I saw how the whole thing was going now. How it goes. She was unfolding. It sucked.

For me, it sucked, anyway, becauseI'm such a good clinger. I can cling to what I love like it's the last morsel of it on earth. One day soon she would be grown and gone and I liked things the way they were, even as hard as it was. I didn't want my baby to grow up. I watered the new tree with my shameful tears of anger and fear and the resentment of the inevitability of life. Even as it felt good, I knew it was so silly. Saying goodbye to what? To who? There is no real goodbye. Not to children. We teach them that, because someone taught it to us. Like we teach a baby to smile.

I saw that through Sophie. She had no innate need to say goodbye. Neither did any of her friends. We adults do, because always in the back of our minds there is the ever-so-slightly realistic fear this could be the last time we see this person. Say goodbye. You never know in this uncertain world. We will see them again soon, hopefully. God willing. But say goodbye. Offer that respectful tip of the hat to the swirling cosmos, until we meet again, that's all for now. Give them a hug, too, for good measure. A nice squeeze as they leave. Never know. Say goodbye!

But Sophie and her friends never would. "It's time to go," I would say, and when they would finally give it up and Sophie would skip her way to me, her friend to her mom, neither offered so much as a glance backward. The abject joy of their time together was simply ended. As Monty Python used to say, "And now the next skit!"

What a cold and uncaring thing to do, I thought for so long. They are born not knowing how to say goodbye! Tiny, uneducated idiots. Go, say goodbye, give her a hug, say you'll see her soon, I would tell Sophie. It will make you feel better, girl. Or me better. And they would do so, awkwardly, half-heartedly, and then run away again.

"Why do I have to say goodbye?" Sophie finally asked me one time. I could only say, "Because that's what we do when we leave somebody," the kind of answer you give when you know you are totally full of it.

In truth, they weren't saying goodbye because, I realized, there was no real goodbye. You never really left, just like you were never really away to begin with. They realize that because they still live it. They are still so close to the beginning that they know there is no goodbye, yet. We are all together all the time. The fear and uncertainty is left for us to pound into them, along with a lot of other misconceptions they had right from the beginning. They can't wipe their own butts, but they can teach us a few of the bigger things. Like, we do not ever really leave.

Someone somewhere said the source of all our unhappiness lies in the illusion that we are separated from others. So far, to me, children are exhibit A.

***Matthew Green** is a free-lance writer and a stay-at-home dad for the past ten years in the Central Coast area of California. Raised in the Midwest, and a film editor in Boston and L.A in his past life, he escaped to spend his time chasing his two little girls and wondering what just happened. Matthew recently finished writing* The Luckiest Man in the World, *a humorous look at being a stay-at-home dad. His active blog can be found at www.worldsluckiestman.com.*

LAST MOMENTS

RJ Licata, East Syracuse, NY

I woke up startled. Joey, my four-year-old son, has been known to walk into our bedroom in the middle of the night. Usually it's because he wakes up and realizes he's alone in his room. He and I don't typically say anything to each other when I hear his feet pitter-patter on our hardwood floor. I just reach one arm over the side of the bed, and he latches on, his favorite blanket in tow. Then, I lift him up into the bed with us. My bed real estate usually suffers some, but I do not mind because it's nice to have him there with us.

This most recent time was different, though. I did not hear him walk in. I must have unconsciously felt his stare, because at around midnight I slowly opened my eyes, and his face was eight inches away from mine, expressionless. After my heart re-started, I went about our usual routine and hoisted him up into our bed between my wife, Dani, and myself. Aside from still being slightly terrified by his creepy entrance (how long was he watching me? 30 seconds? Three minutes? *Longer?*), things settled down pretty quickly and we both started to go back to sleep. That's when the real show began.

We were visited by a thunderstorm, which parked itself directly over our house and performed what sounded like the grand finale of a fireworks show. The flash from the lightning lit our house with enough glow to read by, and the thunder followed immediately after. The house shook, rattling a picture off the dining room wall. Joey wasn't crying, but he did look at me and timidly asked if we were going to have to get a new house when the storm destroyed ours. I told him no, we would not need another house because the storm was likely going to destroy us, as well. No, I'm joking. I told him we, and our house, would be just fine.

After ten minutes or so the storm moved on, content to terrorize other neighborhoods. Our three-year-old Gianna, ever her father's daughter, slept through the entire thing just like I used to do as a kid.

Now, by itself, this thunderstorm story is not much to talk about, but it did trigger a nostalgic thought.

When I was young, say in the 8-12 year-old range, my friends and I would get together for backyard football games, kickball in the street, or nightly hide-and-seek contests. We spent an entire childhood worth of summers doing these things, and then, one day, we reported home for dinner, or curfew (I don't remember which), and that was it. We never played again. I'm not sure which day it was, or why that day became our last. I don't even remember details of that day or game. All I know is I have not played a neighborhood kickball game in close to twenty years.

When that thought first struck me, it made me consider all the other lasts that just kind of happen, completely unbeknownst to us at the time. I'm not talking so much about the big things; those "lasts" tend to leave an impression on us, often because we know it's going to be the last time it happens, like our last high-school football game or the last time we saw our favorite big-leaguer play before he retired.

I began to wonder about the smaller events, the ones that so critically shape our lives before quietly becoming part of our past. Why don't those "lasts" leave a greater impact on us? Why can't I remember the last time we walked home from the sandlot, under the buzzing glow of the streetlights, with grass stains on our knees and tears in our shirts? What was it that finally made us no longer get together for a summer night of hide-and-seek?

Lasts are often sad, but there is something extra sad about the fact that you do not always know they're coming and sometimes you do not remember them at all.

As I mentioned, Joey has a habit of climbing into our bed in the middle of the night. We know, eventually, he will stop. He's not always going to need us in the middle of the night. One night he will come in, and the next time he won't. And he never will again after that.

We won't know it's going to be the last time when it happens. We won't wake up the next morning aware that we will never share our bed with him again. Thunderstorm or not, he will no longer creep into our room in the middle of the night. He won't bring his favorite blanket to my bedside, waiting for my arm to reach down and pull him up. There won't be any announcement. There will be no big farewell tour. One morning we will wake up to a childless bed, and our bed will stay that way for all the mornings to follow.

Just one of many last moments, quietly shaping our lives.

***RJ Licata** is the author of* Lessons for Joey: 100 Things I Can't Wait to Teach My Son. *You can read more of his writing at www.LessonsandLove.com, where he examines the teachable moments in everyday life. RJ lives in East Syracuse, New York with his wife, Danielle, and their three children, Joey, Gianna and Gabrielle.*

CONCLUSION

As we noted in our first book of this series, *Dads Behaving DADLY: 67 Truths, Tears and Triumphs of Modern Fatherhood*, "More and more fathers are asserting themselves and actively taking part in changing diapers, attending doctor's appointments, participating in PTA meetings and helping with homework."

We know this because we have lived it. Hogan was an at-home dad for twenty years; Al is on his thirteenth year. Hogan founded the first Dads Club in California in 1994 and led countless workshops for new dads in hospitals throughout Los Angeles. Both of us have helped organize the last ten Annual At-Home Dads Conventions. Al has been the President of the National At-Home Dad Network for the past four years. We have both appeared in hundreds of interviews about modern fatherhood on television, radio and in print.

We became fathers in the midst of a dramatic cultural shift in parenting. Pew Research found last year that there are now two million stay-at-home dads in the U.S., up from about 1.1 million in 1989. The Boston College Center for Work and Family found that working dads are facing more work/life pressures than moms and over 50 percent of working dads would prefer to be the primary caregiver if their family finances allowed.

As we argued in our first book, these trends will continue because women are continuing to gain momentum in the workforce, allowing "dads to have opportunities and choices they never had before." The U.S. Census reports that 37 percent of women in the U.S. have a bachelor's degree or higher compared to 35 percent of men. According to the Bureau of Labor Statistics, 38 percent of wives out earn their husbands. Some have called this "The End of Men." We believe it is the beginning for men.

With women continuing to gain in the workplace, dads now have the freedom to be the more involved parents they want to be as stay-at-home dads, work-at-home dads, take on a less demanding job or do flex work. These economic factors, however, are only one part of the cultural shift occurring in parenting.

Today's dads, whether they work or are at home, have embraced a larger share of the caregiving and household duties as well as volunteering at schools and becoming involved in fatherhood organizations. According to Pew, 46 percent of today's dads report spending more time with their kids than their fathers spent with them. Pew also found that dads are nearly equal to moms in the number of hours they spend on household duties.

Also more and more dads are joining together to help each other become better dads. Boot Camp for New Dads is offered in hospitals in 45 states. The National Center for Fathering Watch D.O.G.S. program is in 4,595 schools in 46 states. The National At-Home Dad Network, founded in 1995, will host its 20th Annual At-Home Dads Convention in Raleigh, NC this September. Dad 2.0 Summit recently sold out its fifth conference, bringing together dad bloggers and brands interested in reaching dads. City Dads Group, founded in 2008, has dad groups in 16 major U.S. cities and continues to grow.

Dads are coming together to discuss parenting and to find camaraderie. This has allowed today's dads to be more involved with their families and more willing to be emotionally vulnerable about parenting, helping them be better dads.

What we have discovered through our years of advocating for dads and in assembling the books in this series is that the best way for dads to explore their emotional vulnerability is to talk about their feelings in a safe place where they will not be judged. We have witnessed dads talk openly and honestly about the challenges of parenting and then seen the relief on their faces when another dad opens up to explain a similar situation and his feelings as well.

Compiling the stories for this book has been our way to show you what modern fatherhood looks like today, what it will be tomorrow, and to give dads a secure place to explore their own emotions about fatherhood.

We hope you will share some of the stories you have just read in this book with your partner, children, relatives, friends, neighbors, strangers and, most importantly, other dads. We hope the stories you share spark a conversation about a similar incident in your life. We hope the stories allow you to feel safe enough to open up, share your feelings and find a pathway toward feeling better about yourself and your parenting. We hope you will seek out other like-minded dads, start your own local dad group, attend other fatherhood events and read other books about modern fatherhood (a list of our favorites are on our website at www.DadsBehavingDadly.com).

And, most of all, we hope you are inspired to be even more DADLY.

COMING SOON

FROM HOGAN HILLING AND MOTIVATIONAL PRESS

Gay Dads Behaving DADLY:
Truths, Tears and Triumphs of Gay Fatherhood

Dads Behaving DADLY 3:
More Truths, Tears and Triumphs of Modern Fatherhood

Moms Behaving MOMLY:
Women Who Stand Beside DADLY Dads

If you are interested in submitting your DADLY story to our next books, please visit

www.DadsBehavingDadly.com

and follow us

@TheDadGuru

and

@BehavingDadly

ALSO FROM HOGAN HILLING

Dads Behaving DADLY:
67 Truths, Tears and Triumphs of Modern Fatherhood
(Motivational Press, 2014)

When Divorce Do Us Part
(Motivational Press, 2014)

Pacifi(her): What She's Thinking When She's Pregnant
(Turner Publishing, 2011)

Rattled: What He's Thinking When You're Pregnant
(Turner Publishing, 2011)

The Modern Mom's Guide to Dads
(Cumberland House, 2007)

The Man Who Would Be Dad
(Capital Books, 2002)